PRAISE FOR

THE PEACEFUL DAUGHTER'S GUIDE TO SEPARATING FROM A DIFFICULT MOTHER

"The *Peaceful Daughter's Guide* is a practical and uplifting guide for the scores of women whose relationship with their mothers is less than optimal!"

CHRISTIANE NORTHRUP, M.D.
Ob/gyn physician and author of the New York Times bestsellers: *Goddesses Never Age: The Secret Prescription for Radiance, Vitality, and Wellbeing, Women's Bodies, Women's Wisdom,* and *The Wisdom of Menopause*

"The work that Karen Anderson is doing with daughters in regards to their mothers is some of the most important work on the planet today. When we understand how influenced our minds are by what happened when we were growing up, we can then decide to let it go. In this book, Karen gives us the steps to do just that. I know from experience that this work is not easy, but it is by far the most important work I have ever done. Let Karen show you the way."

BROOKE CASTILLO
Master Coach Instructor & Founder of The Life Coach School

"I've been a fan and follower of Karen C.L. Anderson for a long time. She's kind, compassionate, and she so gets it. Kudos to her on more evidence of that with *The Peaceful Daughter's Guide to Separating from a Difficult Mother*. In it, she brings to life how to maneuver through what for many of us is a very difficult yet primary relationship and come out on top—not to the detriment of anyone and much to the benefit of yourself. It's a valuable read for anyone who has or had "mother problems". And there's a bonus: The strategies she suggests could be helpful in any close relationship in your life."

MARSHA HUDNALL
MS, RDN, CD, President & Co-Owner, Green Mountain at Fox Run

THE PEACEFUL DAUGHTER'S GUIDE

TO SEPARATING FROM A DIFFICULT MOTHER

BY KAREN C. L. ANDERSON

COPYRIGHT

Copyright © Karen C.L. Anderson, 2015

All rights reserved. No part of this book may be reproduced in any form without permission in writing from the author. Reviewers may quote brief passages in reviews.

ISBN: 978-1-942646-85-3

Library of Congress Control Number: 2015956703

DISCLAIMER

No part of this publication may be reproduced or transmitted in any form or by any means, mechanical or electronic, including photocopying or recording, or by any information storage and retrieval system, or transmitted by email without permission in writing from the author.

Neither the author nor the publisher assumes any responsibility for errors, omissions, or contrary interpretations of the subject matter herein. Any perceived slight of any individual or organization is purely unintentional.

The author is not a licensed professional. This book details the author's personal experience and opinions. Among other things, it includes the author's reactions and memories. The author acknowledges that others may remember certain situations that she recounts in this book differently than she does. She is aware that others may have experienced some of the situations in the book in a way that is significantly different from the way she portrays them.

Cover Design: John Matthews
Interior Design: Heidi Miller
Editing: Kate Makled

DEDICATION

*This book is for my mother, her mother,
and for all of the generational patterns that need healing.*

TABLE OF CONTENTS

Preface — Living in Either/Or Land

Introduction

1   **Chapter 1:** Awakening

9   **Chapter 2:** "So, tell me about your relationship with your mother?"

13   **Chapter 3:** What's Your Story?

25   **Chapter 4:** But What About the Anger/Sadness/Grief/Bitterness I Still Feel?

39   **Chapter 5:** Triggers + Buttons + Thorns, OH MY!

47   **Chapter 6:** Deactivate Your Triggers, Unbutton Your Buttons + Pluck Out Those Thorns

57   **Chapter 7:** Do No Harm, but Take No Shit: How to Set Empowered Boundaries

71   **Chapter 8:** But Mothers Aren't Supposed to…

77   **Chapter 9:** Mother As A Verb, Not A Noun

87   **Chapter 10:** When You Decide to Change

93	**Chapter 11:** Choosing to Love Your Mother Unconditionally, as the Greatest Gift You Can Give Yourself (A How-To Guide)
99	**Chapter 12:** What's on the Other Side of the Struggle?
105	**Chapter 13:** How Does This Book End?
111	**The Peaceful Daughter Manifesto**
115	**An Open Letter To Your Mother**
119	**Recommended Resources**
123	**Acknowledgements**
125	**About the Author**
129	**Thank You**

PREFACE —
LIVING IN EITHER/OR LAND

> *Liberation is the ability to see multiple options. No matter how silly a circumstance may sound, if it gives you the ability to widen your perspective, it helps set you free.*
>
> **MARTHA BECK**

When it comes to your relationship with your mother, does it often feel like an all-or-nothing, either/or proposition? Maybe you feel that you have to either be defensive, resistant, and protective of yourself, or instead just roll over and let her do and say whatever she wants.

Or maybe it feels like you either have to keep your conversations shallow and surface-y or go right into the emotional deep end.

Then there are times when you think you either have to shut her out of your life — for good — or allow yourself to be enmeshed with her forever.

None of these options feel good. In fact, just *thinking* about it wears you out.

Having felt this way in my relationship with my own mother, and having worked with other women on this very issue, I find it's more common than you may know to feel this way…and it sucks.

At the very least, it's slightly annoying or limiting. At the very worst, it's intense and can feel as debilitating as impotent rage. And underlying all of it is sadness, maybe there is unspoken grief.

I spent years in either/or land. Way back when, if someone had told me that it didn't have to be this way, I'd have simply said, "You don't know my mother." It felt like an intractable situation, with no pleasant solution.

Now I know better. I know that there are infinite choices available, not just all-or-nothing decisions. There's immense freedom, peace, and empowerment that comes with knowing that, along with being confident in making choices that feel good and right (and when I say that, I don't mean making choices for your mother's sake, for avoiding conflict, or for her approval).

So when it comes to your relationship with your mother, this I know for sure: You are not as powerless as you feel, and you can make choices that feel good and free.

INTRODUCTION

I wrote this book because I, too, have a mother story — a story that I am freeing myself from every day. Of all the hard things I've ever done, this has been the hardest — and most rewarding, powerful and freeing.

That is my number one credential. I have been there. And I'm *not* there anymore.

So what can you expect? This book is part lessons and concepts, part real-life experience. It's also part journal prompts and exercises that will help you apply the lessons and concepts and make them real in your own life.

I suggest you keep a journal specifically for this work. Why? Because writing is powerful and it's good for you. Writing about stressful events helps you acknowledge, cope with, and resolve them, which has a positive impact on your physical health.

(To make the process even easier, you can download and print the *free* Peaceful Daughter Workbook, which includes all the journal prompts and exercises: http://worksheets.kclanderson.com.)

Writing also helps you to:

Clarify your thoughts and feelings. As you get deeper into the book you will understand the difference between the two.

Know yourself better. What makes you happy and confident? What situations and people are challenging?

Reduce stress. Writing about uncomfortable thoughts and emotions is the beginning of being able to release them.

Solve problems from a more intuitive, creative place. Writing unlocks creativity and intuition, and unleashes unexpected solutions.

> *...creativity is such a powerful integration tool. Creating is the act of paying attention to our experiences and connecting the dots so we can learn more about ourselves and the world around us. ... we just need to do a little writing — nothing formal, just jotting down some notes on our experiences.*
>
> **BRENÉ BROWN**

It takes courage to do this work. Intense emotions may come up as you make your way through the book. You could find yourself feeling everything from guilt to anger to grief, but also joy, hilarity, and relief.

How you feel about your mother right now is okay. Although there may be societal, cultural, and family taboos in regards to the emotions we experience (especially if they are deemed "negative") there are no taboos — or judgment — here.

The key is to engage with compassionate objectivity and examine yourself with fascination and curiosity, rather than harsh judgment, shame, and guilt.

JOURNAL PROMPT:
WHAT'S YOUR INTENTION?

To break in your journal (or workbook), I invite you to consider your intention for yourself as you work your way through this book. No matter where you are in your relationship with your mother, whether she is alive or not, whether you speak to her or not, consider three things when coming up with your intention:

How you'd like to feel on a day-to-day basis.

What you'd like your relationship with your mother to look like*

Who you want to be.

*I am not suggesting that you *should* want it to look a certain way, like for example, the two of you skipping, hand in hand, into the sunset...unless that's what *you* really want. There is *no* right answer for this question.

This work is more about *you* than her.

How do you know if you have mother issues? Here are some common ways they show up:

You compare and despair.

You feel stuck, overwhelmed, and like an under-achiever.

Or you are over-achieving, but without any joy or fulfillment, just going through the motions in an effort to prove your worth.

Shame, blame, guilt, and desperation.

Fear of failure.

Fear of success (believe it or not): believing that if you *succeed* you won't be loved, someone will disapprove, or that you're somehow "showing off."

Putting up with "bad behavior" in others.

Constantly seeking approval, validation, and permission from outside yourself (and especially from your mother).

People-pleasing and being afraid to say "no."

Taking on other people's problems and thinking it's on you to fix them.

Self-sabotage (especially when you get close to achieving something).

Binge eating, binge drinking, binge shopping, binge *anything*.

Trying to control the uncontrollable.

Chronic worry and anxiety.

Believing that it is selfish or narcissistic to put yourself first, or even to love, accept, or care for yourself.

Believing it is your responsibility to take care of others, emotionally speaking.

Thinking that your desires and preferences don't matter.

Not having a clear sense of who you are and what you want.

And if you DO know what you want, feeling incapable of doing or having it.

Having weak or non-existent boundaries.

Afraid to speak your truth and take up space.

If you identify with any or all of these, it's not bad news, although it may feel that way right now. You may have accepted (or struggled to accept) that this is just the way you are — that it's set in stone and unchangeable. Or maybe you understand that you *can* change it, but it feels overwhelming and near impossible to do so. Besides, it's not like you ever had a great role model for being the woman you *want* to be. I used to feel the same way, until I learned the concepts I am about to lay out in this book.

GOT QUESTIONS? I HAVE ANSWERS

Does my mother have to be alive in order for me to get something out this?

NO! This book and the lessons, concepts, and exercises aren't so much about *the two of you* as they are about you making some choices about how you want to show up in the world. This is about your future, and not just in relation to your mother (whether she's alive or not).

I don't want to have to talk to/see/interact with my mother. Are you going to suggest that I should?

Absolutely not. For some women, choosing to not have their mothers in their lives is the very best choice. What I want for you is to have made choices from a loving, proactive, empowered place, not from a reactive, defensive place.

My mother was abusive and violent when I was a child. Am I supposed to forgive and forget?

This book isn't about putting up with or approving of any type of abuse, whether it happened long ago or is happening now. It's about learning how to tell the story about what happened in such a way that it doesn't hurt or minimize you now, but rather empowers and liberates you. It's about learning how to establish loving, empowered boundaries so you can put a stop to the abuse, if it is still happening.

I've taken everyone else's advice for years to no end. You can't possibly know my mother!

My job isn't to tell you what to do. My intention is simply to guide you in having your own back...in learning how to trust yourself implicitly when it comes to your relationship with your mother — or anyone else.

CHAPTER 1

AWAKENING

The image is vivid in my memory. My mother is standing in the front yard and she's holding a letter in her hand — a letter she's about to put in the mailbox.

She holds it up, and forcefully says, "I'm divorcing my mother."

At the time, I was in my early 20s and my mother was in her mid-40s. I certainly wasn't surprised; it was no secret that she and my grandmother didn't get along. My mother often said that she would never treat me the way her mother had treated her. I'd heard the stories and they made me hurt for my mother.

At the time, my mother and I had what I thought to be "typical" mother-daughter conflict, but I also thought our relationship was different. My mother often said that we were close…good friends, even. I know she *wanted* it to be different between us than it had been for her with her own mother.

What I didn't know at the time was that my mother and I were not "close," we were codependent and enmeshed.

Fast-forward 25 years, and there I was, divorcing my mother, too. Instead of a letter in the mail, it was me sending an email. Although it wasn't the same patterns as the earlier generation, my mother and I didn't have a healthy relationship, either. My mother had unconsciously passed down attitudes and behaviors, I unconsciously took them, and when I wanted to strike out on my own and have a separate life from my mother, our relationship became difficult, as well.

The details are not important. Sure, I could tell you about all the things that led up to that moment — to justify "divorcing" my mother — but all that's important to know is that at the time I felt like I had no other option.

That was at the end of 2010.

I believed that divorcing my mother — choosing to have no contact with her — would solve all my problems.

Instead, I found myself obsessing about our relationship. To anyone who would listen, I'd pour out my hurt and anger, sharing the details of how my mother had done me wrong. What I didn't know at the time is that deep down inside, I believed I was my mother's victim. So I acted like one.

When I discovered the concept of "victim consciousness," it all made sense. Up until that point, I resisted the idea that I might be a victim. In my family, "being a victim" was something to be ashamed of.

I highly recommend the work of Lynne Forrest and her book, *Beyond Victim Consciousness*, for fully understanding this concept, but let me lay out the basics here.

Imagine an inverted triangle. At the bottom of the triangle is the Victim, in the top left corner is the Persecutor, and in the top right corner is the Rescuer (note that both these roles are in the "one up" position from the Victim). When we're in victim consciousness, we're playing one of those three roles, and it's important to recognize that none of these roles is considered better than other (especially when everyone in the dynamic is an adult). The Rescuer is *not* the "good guy."

According to Forrest: "Victims think of themselves as weak and unable to take care of themselves so they are constantly on the lookout for someone to rescue them. Rescuers tend to believe that their own needs are irrelevant. They believe that they matter only when they are taking care of others, and that means they constantly need someone to take care of. Persecutors believe the world is a generally unsafe and fearful place. They think of themselves as being in constant need of protection from a world that is out to get them, and so they get angry at others or at situations believing that they are only defending themselves."

No matter where you start out on the triangle, you will eventually play the other two roles. If you're the Victim, you start to feel resentment, and may even move into the Persecutor role in order to change the pattern, believing you are protecting yourself. Or, you may move into the Rescuer role in order to feel important because you're taking care of the Victim.

In hindsight, I see that my mother and I constantly revolved around the triangle, each of us playing all three roles. Even when I was a tiny baby, I was playing all three roles.

It is possible to take yourself out of victim consciousness entirely, and I will explain what that means further in Chapter 6.

Coincidently (or not), shortly after my "divorce" from my mother, I became my maternal grandmother's legal guardian.

When it became obvious that she'd no longer be able to live alone in her home, I moved her into a skilled nursing facility, cleaned out her house, and sold it. It was while readying her house for sale that I found a series of letters she and my mother had written to each other, from the time my mother was 18.

I treasured those letters because they gave me so much insight. They mirror, almost exactly, some of the correspondence my mother and I have exchanged over the years. In some cases, the letters conveyed basic day-to-day observations and news, but others were filled with rage, hurt, accusations, and confusion.

I even found the infamous "I'm divorcing you" letter my mother sent my grandmother.

My point in sharing this story is to illustrate that despite what we say, despite what we might intend, what we model is what makes the biggest impact. I'm not saying I divorced my mother because she divorced hers, nor am I saying that what either of us did during that time was right (or wrong).

Dysfunctional patterns, if not noticed and acknowledged honestly, get passed on. Although I chose not to have children, I saw the effects of those patterns in some of my other relationships, too, from my marriage, to my sister (same father, different mother), to my step kids.

It wasn't pretty. I was harsh, critical, and downright mean sometimes. And I believed I was justified. I was treating others the way I had been treated…and the way I had treated myself. Being "in conflict" was the norm for me. It's a constant that I was used to.

I'm not blaming my mother, or her mother, for the patterns. What I know now is that what was passed down was the pain of "not good enough." In some circles, it's called the "mother wound," and it's literally the pain of being a woman in a patriarchal society — the pain of harsh self-judgment, criticism, and unworthiness, that has been passed down, woman to woman, mother to daughter, for centuries.

By itself, that pain is one of the most significant sources of dysfunction in our relationships. Those beliefs and patterns are running in the background of our lives, and we often have no clue that they're there at all. We just know that we're not as content as we'd like to be. Our relationships aren't fulfilling and rich. Everything else just seems "normal."

The good news is that we don't have to take what is handed down. It's not something to blame our mothers, fathers (or ourselves) for, it's something to understand, accept, and work on. Meanwhile, we come to know that we can do hard work without suffering — that it can be one of the most joyful, affirming things we ever do.

By being honest and aware of how, at first, I chose to believe that I was not good enough, I opened the door to healing. In deciding that I didn't want to believe it any more, I released it, not just for me, but also for my mother, her mother, and on and on, and walked through that door.

Doing this work heals — not just you, and not just in the present — but also past generations (although I believe doing it just for you is perfectly okay). It also changes the future. It sets up a healing vibration that ripples forward to those around you, your children, and out into the world.

And that is the number one reason to take an honest and compassionate look at your relationship with your mother, and ask yourself what you've chosen to take from her, what you're passing on, and if it's not what you choose, then heal it.

World peace does indeed start inside each and every one of us.

CHAPTER 2:

"SO, TELL ME ABOUT YOUR RELATIONSHIP WITH YOUR MOTHER?"

Classic, right? It's what every therapist I've ever seen, traditional or alternative, has (eventually) asked when I sought help for various issues (from weight loss to anxiety).

And then, there are all the books I've read. Books like *Mothers Who Can't Love: A Healing Guide For Daughters*, by Dr. Susan Forward and *Will I Ever Be Good Enough: Healing The Daughters Of Narcissistic Mothers*, by Dr. Karyl McBride.

While I found great comfort in telling my story to therapists, and in realizing that I am not alone when I read those books, none of this insight or experience did anything to bring me true and lasting freedom and peace.

Very often therapy and "self help" provides an excuse to stay a lesser version of your possible self. They provide context for pathology, but don't always give us a path toward healing and being able to feel whole. In some ways, they promote an "acceptance" that limits our growth and potential. Until we learn it doesn't have to be that way.

That's not to say that therapy and books weren't helpful or didn't play an important role, because they most certainly were and did for me. In fact, I'd say they were key parts of the process.

It was a relief to have an explanation, but at first I found myself even more validated in feeling angry, sad, bitter, disappointed, and reactive. For a while, it was rather exhilarating. What I didn't realize is that I went deeper into an unhealthy "blame" mode than I ever had before, because I had adopted a deep-seated unconscious belief: *It shouldn't have been that way.*

My mother shouldn't have been the way she was, I shouldn't have been the way I was, my parents shouldn't have gotten divorced, and all the bad things that happened in the past shouldn't have happened.

There is no freedom or peace in *shoulds and shouldn'ts*. I just didn't know any other way! While I didn't like feeling angry, sad, bitter, disappointed, and reactive, those emotions were validated by experts, therapists, and books (and friends and family), so I thought I had a good reason to feel them. (And I did, but not *for the rest of my life!*).

Besides, there's nothing wrong with feeling so-called negative emotions. It's actually imperative that we DO feel them (and I will show you how to do that in Chapter 4). In fact, grief — for the past, for yourself, for what you never had but wished you did — is completely natural and normal. It's "clean" pain, at least the first time you fully feel it.

Here's the big *but*: When you're chronically angry, sad, bitter, disappointed, and reactive, perhaps you don't perceive that you're responsible for those emotions. You believe you either don't have a choice, or that you're being *made* to feel them — by your mother. You find yourself stuck and unable to move beyond this pain, so you tell these stories over and over again.

It may seem foreign to you right now, but consider that you can have compassion for yourself as you grieve, and as you process all those other negative emotions. Moving through it is the only way to the other side of it.

Is it scary? Hell yes. It may seem cliché for me to say, "If I can do it, you can too," but that is the truth. There was a time when I saw myself as completely broken, unfixable, and, well, doomed. Doomed to a life of mediocrity. I was wrong. *So* wrong.

CHAPTER 3:

WHAT'S YOUR STORY?

> *We now know that memories are not fixed or frozen, like Proust's jars of preserves in a larder, but are transformed, disassembled, reassembled, and recategorized with every act of recollection.*
>
> **OLIVER SACKS**, NEUROLOGIST AND WRITER

Every woman has a mother story. A story she uses to define herself, to limit herself, to react from, to blame from, and to shame herself from.

Stories like:

"I'm not good enough!"

"I can't have what I want."

"It doesn't matter what I want."

"I don't know what I want."

"I wish someone would just tell me what to do."

"I'm overwhelmed."

"I can't help it."

"I'm so stressed out!!"

"I'll take care of myself later."

"Who do I think I am?"

"I can't say no."

"I'm a control freak...that's just the way I am."

"If I don't do it, she will be mad!"

"She pisses me off!"

"How much more do I have to do?"

If you identify with any, most, or all of these, the good news is — you are not alone! Actually, *none* of this is bad news. It doesn't mean you're weak, pathetic, or a loser. It doesn't mean that you're anything short of an amazing, powerful woman right this very minute. It just means that you've got a belief pattern that is looping in your brain: in other words, a story.

What you're going to do, as you work through this book, is examine your story. Ultimately, you will free yourself from it, so you can come home to yourself as an autonomous, empowered, resilient woman. You will be accumulating moments of consciousness and allowing yourself to practice concepts that will eventually become part of who you are. Let's dig in...

> *Owning our story and loving ourselves through that process is the bravest thing that we will ever do.*
>
> **BRENÉ BROWN**

I used to think that owning my story meant telling anyone who would listen about all the things my mother did to me. When I came across this quote, I wondered why Brené said it was brave, because I didn't feel brave. I usually felt a combination of vindication and guilt.

I didn't realize what it meant to truly own my story (and I will share more about what that actually means later on in this chapter), but once I did, I started to understand what Brené meant when she said it is the bravest thing we'll ever do.

So what is a story? It's best to make the distinction this way: there's what happened (the facts) and then there's *what we've made it mean*, specifically about us and our mothers. *That* is the story.

What matters most about our stories is the way in which we tell them and the meaning we derive from them. By our very nature, humans create meaning. Since meaning comes with looking back, we have the opportunity to make meaning that either holds us back or supports our growth. Our stories always have the potential to do *both*.

> *We can look back and tell our stories through the lens of defeat, coming up with examples of giving up, drowning in grief, missed opportunities, coming to the purpose of our lives far too late in life to do anything truly extraordinary with them.*
>
> *Or, we can we could look back and tell our stories through the lens of courage. We can just as easily see that we were steadfast and positively stubborn in our persistence, that we never ever gave up, that we plodded forward even when it felt like we were in mud up to our knees, and that we finally finally were brave enough to claim our purpose and that in doing so, at this time in our lives, we became an example to others that it is never ever too late to begin again.*
>
> **WENDI KELLY**

Most women have stories they tell others about their mothers. Some of the stories are about their childhoods, and others are more recent. Here are some of the stories my clients have told me:

"She abused me."

"She is an alcoholic."

"She was depressed."

"She neglected me."

"She's a narcissist."

"She makes fun of me."

"She slept with my boyfriend."

"She always ruins Thanksgiving."

"She's aways late."

And so on.

Here is the way I used to tell my mother story:

My parents got divorced when I was three and my mother got remarried to a violent alcoholic. They both drank too much and they were abusive to me and to each other. I grew up in a chaotic, violent household.

My mother was also very controlling of me and put me on diets even though I wasn't really overweight. She was jealous of me. And as I got older, it just got worse.

She had no boundaries and because I had no clue who I was (because she controlled me), I just let her continue to run my life. Every time I tried to strike out my own, she either guilted me back into line or threatened or criticized. I never felt like I could make a move without my mother's approval. And when I tried to do something I loved, she'd criticize it.

I started binge eating. I gained weight, I had a series of bad relationships with men. I have to either hate her or be her door mat. I don't want it to be this way, but I have to protect myself. Basically I have no self-esteem and my life has sucked because of my mother.

I finally cut her out of my life a few years ago, thinking that everything would be much easier, but it hasn't been. I am wracked with guilt most of the time...and fear too. But a lot of the time I feel white hot, impotent anger.

You might be thinking, "But Karen, if those things happened, you have a right to be angry! You have a right to feel the way you do." And sure, I was a helpless victim at one point in my life. But my story didn't empower me! My story kept me stuck.

How? Because of the unconscious painful beliefs I had about me, as a result. These are some of the painful stories I told myself, about myself:

I am powerless.

I should be ashamed.

I am ashamed.

I have no idea what I want.

She knows what's best.

Being who I am isn't okay.

My body is wrong.

Anything I might want for me is also hers.

I am stupid.

I am irresponsible.

I don't know any better.

I am helpless.

I am pathetic.

I am too much.

I am too big for my britches.

I can never win.

I can't take care of myself.

I can't trust myself.

I can't trust her.

I am bad, silly, or stupid, unless I am doing what she thinks I should do.

I am selfish.

What I feel isn't real.

I don't know what I really feel.

My feelings should be shut down.

That is what I was telling myself, about me. That's what I made all of that other stuff mean. Here comes the brave part: *I did that to myself. I created that story and I hurt myself with it.*

It might have been something I naturally learned from my experiences. It might be what was modeled by both my mother and my grandmother. It might have started as something someone who should have loved me was "doing to me."

But I didn't *have* to internalize all that — or enforce it on myself, *forever*. It wouldn't create the possibility for my life to ever be different, or for all that I truly could become, to actualize.

When I owned it, when I realized that I had been doing it to myself, I was deeply ashamed. I can feel the prickle of shame on my face even now, just writing about it.

And then? I realized how deeply powerful I am.

I had spent years in therapy (not to mention all the time spent reading those books about mothers who can't love and narcissistic mothers), wallowing around in my sad story, and continuing to feel stuck, powerless, and believing that — because of my past — I wouldn't be able to change.

What you're about to do isn't a matter of digging around in your past and wallowing in sad stories. You're about to embark on a joyful journey, from where you are, right now.

That said, I do get it. I get that there are issues from the past — issues concerning your mother — issues that might go all the way back to when you were born, or even before that! I also get that they feel fixed and permanent. We tend to adopt an "I am less than" persona when we have mother issues, because it keeps us safe in a twisted way. We allow ourselves to be dependent, and we allow others to dictate who we're allowed to be, in order to receive what we believe "love" is (i.e. our mother's approval). It's important to acknowledge and honor those issues and the stories we've told about them ever since.

So what you're going to do in this first lesson (which I adapted from a similar lesson Iyanla Vanzant did on an episode of the Oprah Winfrey Network) is tell your story in the way that you may be used to telling it. Then you're going to transform it in a way that will *empower you* rather than leave you feeling hopeless and stuck.

Time to pull out your journal (or your Peaceful Daughter Workbook)...

JOURNAL PROMPT:
TELL YOUR STORY

Step 1: Write down your story in as much detail as you can. What your mother did or didn't do; what your mother should have done; what she shouldn't have done; how your life would have been different if only thus-and-such hadn't happened; how you'd be thinner, happier, richer if only [fill in the blank] hadn't happened; what you did or didn't have because [fill in the blank]. Write it *all* down. Even if it takes pages and pages, get the whole thing out of your head.

Step 2: Pare it down to the point where you can tell the story in as few words as possible (with the goal being less than 10 words total). The key here is to boil it down to the very bare facts: nothing more, nothing less, and with no opinion or judgment placed on it.

Step 3: Ask yourself what you made your mother story mean about you. What are the things you told yourself, about yourself, in response to your story? Write all these things down.

Step 4: Now list the things you do (or don't do) because of how you *feel* about your story.

Step 5: Now describe what your life looks like as a result of what you do or don't do. How do you show up in your life?

Step 6: Now sum up your story, which includes these elements:

Your story in 10 words or less. For example: ("I am _____" or "_____ happened")

How you feel in response to your story (what you made it mean about you). For example, "I acknowledge that there's a part of me that feels _____ because _____."

What you do to hide or deny those feelings.

What your life looks like because you hide or deny your feelings.

Step 7: Can you forgive yourself for the things you told yourself, about yourself, that aren't really true about you? (This is the stuff you made it mean.).

Step 8: Are you willing to give up that story?

From here, you can start to redefine who you are now, as an emotionally adult woman, not as a little girl. What is it that you want for yourself and your life? An important distinction here: don't magnify the "againstness" (emphasizing what you don't want, who you don't want to be) without knowing what it is you *do* want. With a clear definition of what you want and what you expect for your life, you can begin to create and set boundaries *from a place of love for yourself*, versus having to react defensively or construct your entire life around avoiding negative experiences.

CHAPTER 4

BUT WHAT ABOUT THE ANGER/SADNESS/GRIEF/BITTERNESS I STILL FEEL?

In the previous chapter we discussed stories — their effect on us, and how we can start to let those stories go. Before we move on to telling ourselves more empowering stories, let's talk about emotions.

The first exercise may have brought up some intense, uncomfortable, and probably unwanted emotions. When those kinds of emotions come up, we tend to be in a hurry to get rid of them. This means we "act" without allowing ourselves to fully feel, express, and most importantly, see what they are trying to teach us.

When you can make room for painful emotions, actively accept them, and not be in a hurry to change them, you learn something that you wouldn't have otherwise learned. We have a tendency to think that if we allow ourselves to feel painful emotions, they will never go away and they will overtake us. In fact, the *opposite* is true.

So, what are emotions? Emotions are energy in motion — vibrations in our bodies that we can feel physically. And they are usually described in one word.

Happy. Sad. Angry. Scared. Happiness has a vibration. Anger has a vibration. Sadness has a vibration. Fear has a vibration.

Emotions are not thoughts or ideas. They are not concepts with long, vague descriptions. They are not opinions or judgments.

The way emotions feel in my body may be different than the way they feel in your body. Sometimes emotional vibrations are uncomfortable, physically, but one thing I know for sure is that allowing myself to feel an uncomfortable emotion has never, ever hurt me. The earth didn't open up and swallow me whole, nor did I explode into a million pieces.

And while emotions themselves are not thoughts or ideas, in the vast majority of cases they come from our thoughts. Something happens, our brains assess what happened, and assign meaning to it. That meaning then informs how we feel. All of this happens in an instant without our awareness.

Here's a pertinent example. A few years ago, my mother sent me an email asking a question about my grandmother's (her mother) trust. I immediately became angry. Seething even. The reason I became angry isn't because of what she said, it's because of what I made her question mean. I made it mean that I am an incapable, stupid, lazy-ass.

That's how it works: something happens, we think a thought about it, assign a meaning to it, and voila, the feeling arises from the thought. The more often we repeat these thoughts and feelings, the more automatic and "hard wired" the emotional processing happens. It becomes a habit for our minds. How very "efficient" of them.

Now let's talk about *how to feel* an emotion. Every human being has the capacity and the capability to literally feel every human emotion. Even the ugly, icky ones. We're built to feel all of them, so it stands to reason that we're capable of feeling them without harming ourselves. Our bodies are great at feeling emotions, and they are amazingly efficient at it. You'll notice that it's impossible to feel an intense emotion for a long time. Our bodies and our brains won't even let that happen.

Consider the story of Dr. Jill Bolte Taylor, a neurologist who had a stroke. In her book, *My Stroke Of Insight*, she describes that after her stroke, she was unable to resist feeling emotions. Without that capacity, and retaining her curiosity about the human mind, she found that for her, an unresisted emotion would last about 90 seconds.

We feel surges of love. Surges of anger. Surges of grief. And then they recede. Even an emotion as intense as grief or anger gives us break. Sure, they come around again, and as long as we let them flow on through, they will again recede.

But sometimes, because we're afraid to feel a feeling — or because we think certain emotions are bad or wrong — the fear intensifies the already uncomfortable emotion. When we resist, say, anger, we create more anger. We get angry at our anger. We worry about our anxiety. We hate our hate. We create more pain by telling ourselves we shouldn't be in pain. We don't want to feel that uncomfortable feeling!

And so, because we assigned a negative meaning to emotions like anger or jealousy, we tend to spend a lot of time avoiding, stuffing, distracting, and intellectualizing these emotions — so we don't have to feel the vibrations — because we consider them ugly and uncomfortable.

Now, consider the difference between resisting a so-called negative feeling and just letting it vibrate. Some people call it "sitting with your emotions." Imagine that you're about to experience an emotion you find uncomfortable, like panic or terror, but you will only experience it for two minutes. Once the two minutes is up, you're done. What would it be like to just *experience* it? Without avoidance, resistance, numbing? What might you notice?

This is what I mean when I talk about safely *feeling* an emotion. And yes, it takes practice, but it's fascinating to experiment with this.

The more you experiment with feeling your feelings, the more you will learn from them. Even better, when you focus on literally feeling the emotion in your body, the faster it goes away! The more you practice sitting with *feeling* icky emotions, the easier it gets.

I figure, if your body is capable of feeling all the emotions, then all feelings are valid and worthy of being felt. They're all useful. They all have messages or even lessons for you.

Now let's talk about safely *expressing* feelings, which includes verbal and non-verbal expression. It's interesting to watch little children express emotion.

Think about an angry or distraught toddler who throws herself to the floor, kicks her legs and flings her arms. What she is doing is letting her body feel and express the emotion. Or if she's sad, she cries, sobbing and shaking, using her whole body. The same goes for expressing joy, with a full-body laugh! Our culture and our families down through the generations have taught us, however, that some emotions are bad — or at least that certain expressions of certain emotions are bad and wrong.

For instance, we teach toddlers that the grocery store floor isn't the best place to express anger. And somewhere along the way, we also learn that some *people* don't like the way we express certain emotions. If we want attention, love, or approval from them, we quickly learn to stop expressing these emotions, or maybe even feeling them altogether. And sometimes we see someone (our mothers?) expressing an emotion we deem ugly, and we decide we don't want to be like them!

So how do you safely express emotion? Especially an emotion like anger, which can also feel dangerous? It's important to remember that feeling anger (or other so-called "negative" emotions) does not make you a bad or "un-evolved" person. You are never "above" having feelings. Emotions like anger become a problem if we pick up a knife and stab someone with it because we're angry. Or if we scream at them. It's okay to let it take as long as it needs to take to feel your pain. It's *not* okay to treat people poorly while you're doing it.

It's more profound to allow yourself to acknowledge and feel it rather than saying, "I'm past that." Usually, when we say that, we're only trying to convince ourselves. I'm also not talking about avoiding/stuffing/distracting/intellectualizing emotions so they become unconscious or chronic, which is how you hurt yourself; or about complaining and wallowing and stewing, which is really another way of resisting emotion.

So let's say you've just noticed that you're sad or angry about something that has happened recently. I'll use an example from my own life.

A while back, my husband and I had a minor argument that escalated into raised voices with both of us wanting to be right about something. This is unusual for us. I noticed, pretty much right away, that I had some anger going on underneath. I realized it was anger that had nothing to do with the subject. As I said, I've practiced this a lot! It wasn't all that long ago that a situation like this would have derailed me, and I would have felt totally out of control with anger.

So the first step is noticing. I noticed the vibration. I focused on how it felt, and I let myself sit with it. Next, you want to acknowledge it. Say it out loud. "I'm angry. I'm pissed. I'm frustrated." Put some feeling into it! Don't forget to breathe. Continue to feel the vibration. And start moving your body in a way that feels natural.

When I am angry, I like to stomp my feet and pump my arms up and down. In the situation with my husband, I chose to go for a walk with loud, intense music playing on my iPhone, and I pumped my arms and muttered under my breath. There have been other times when I chose to stomp around my basement and yell. And yet other times, when I went outside, threw rocks, and swore.

Cry if you need to cry. Scream if you need to scream. Punch a pillow. Take a walk. Swear out loud if it helps. Throw rocks. Let it take as long as it needs to take. This emotion, or energy in motion, will start to dissipate naturally. And probably pretty quickly, depending on how old it is.

Now, you can be curious and fascinated about what you just experienced. Ask yourself what message your emotion had for you. As with most intense emotion, the message is usually from the past, and the emotion that we're feeling isn't new. It's old emotion that we've stuffed. And something triggered it. So now we've had an opportunity to heal.

And finally, take responsibility for your emotions. It may seem counter-intuitive at first, like, "Wait, my husband *made* me angry. He wasn't listening and he wasn't agreeing with me." But the fact of the matter is, my anger is my anger, not his. I'm the one feeling it, and I am the one responsible for the safe expression of it.

Now, that's not to say that I didn't talk to my husband about it later, after I expressed it on my own. I did, but after processing and fully feeling that anger, I was able to speak calmly and without blaming him. Talk about being empowered! It was an amazing experience.

So you're probably thinking, "Wait…I'm supposed to remember all of that the next time I get pissed off?" Nope! It's not all going to happen naturally and automatically, right off the bat. It's a practice, not a perfect. This is something that you become aware of and try out. A little at a time.

> *Each emotion, when it is welcomed in the full village of a resourceful psyche, can signal the presence of an imbalance. Then, each properly channeled emotion will contribute the specific information and intensity needed to alleviate that imbalance and heal the psyche. Once the healing has been achieved, the emotion will move on, as all emotions should. When the emotions are welcomed and their messages can be translated in honorable ways, they are no longer dangerously primal; instead they become brilliant and unceasing energies with which true healing and enlightenment can be achieved.*
>
> **KARLA MCLAREN**, THE AUTHOR OF *THE LANGUAGE OF EMOTION*

The ugly, icky emotions we may have surrounding our relationships with our mothers aren't necessarily going to go away. In fact, it is a very safe bet they will not go away on their own. We can learn to feel and express them safely, without hurting ourselves or our mothers.

This isn't a book you will finish, and find all you're going to feel afterward is happy-happy-joy-joy (and if you don't feel that, you're getting it wrong). Nothing is further from the truth.

This process is about allowing yourself to become emotionally fluent; to understand where your feelings are actually coming from, and develop ways of managing them safely.

Allowing yourself to feel your feelings is the ultimate act of mothering yourself — of holding the space for yourself in a way that, perhaps, your mother couldn't or wouldn't do.

Time to get out your journal (or your Peaceful Daughter Workbook)...

JOURNAL PROMPT:
GET IN TOUCH WITH YOUR FEELINGS

What are you feeling now?

How do you know that you are feeling it?

Where is this feeling in your body?

What color is this feeling?

Is this feeling hard or soft?

Is this feeling fast or slow?

What else can you say about how it feels?

How does this feeling make you want to react?

What judgments do you have about this feeling?

Why are you feeling this?

What is the thought or belief that is causing you to have this feeling?

JOURNAL PROMPT:
HOW DOES YOUR MOTHER MAKE YOU FEEL?

Think about a time when you believed that your mother caused you to have a negative feeling and write down what she did or said:

Describe how she "made" you feel.

Describe why you think she has the power to create your feelings in this way.

Describe your feeling without the influence of your mother (what you would be feeling if she hadn't "made" you feel this way).

What is the thought you are thinking that is causing this feeling?

JOURNAL PROMPT:
EMOTIONS YOU ASSOCIATE WITH YOUR MOTHER AND/OR YOUR RELATIONSHIP

Here are some of the words women who work with me use to describe their relationship with their mothers. I am sure you could come up with many more.

Ashamed

Confused

Hurt

Discouraged

White-hot anger

Afraid

Sad

Guilty

Love

Hate

Helpless/hopeless

Grief

Make a list of the emotions you associate with your relationship with your mother in your journal. For each one, actually take the time to summon up the vibration in your body, and describe it. Play with it, and notice how you can increase it and decrease it at will.

It's important to note that there are several emotion-like words that are actually not emotions, but rather opinions or interpretations. Here are some of those words (with thanks to Marshall Rosenberg and his book, *Nonviolent Communication: A Language Of Life*:

abandoned, abused, attacked, betrayed, boxed-in, bullied, cheated, coerced, cornered, diminished, distrusted, interrupted, intimidated, manipulated, misunderstood, neglected, pressured, provoked, put down, rejected, unappreciated, unheard, unseen, unsupported, unwanted, used

These words do not express emotion, they describe thoughts, opinion, and interpretation, which, *when you choose them*, create emotion. They express how you interpret others, rather than how you feel. This is a crucially important distinction to make, because this is how you start to take back your power!

CHAPTER 5

TRIGGERS + BUTTONS + THORNS, OH MY!

One of my favorite lessons of all time comes from Michael Singer, author of *The Untethered Soul*. It goes like this:

There once was a woman who had a thorn in her arm and that thorn directly touched a nerve. Anything that touched the thorn created pain inside her. Even a leaf brushing against it caused pain.

So, even though she loved to take walks in the woods she stopped doing that. She started avoiding the woods, or anything that might touch the thorn.

She built her life around protecting that thorn, believing that's how she would protect herself from pain. What she didn't realize is that she had another option: to remove the damned thorn.

We all have these thorns (or buttons, triggers…whatever you want to call them), and we don't want anybody to touch, push, or pull them. And if someone does, we get all upset, because no one should have touched our thorn. We train people not to touch our thorns, and we build a life around not getting hurt.

"Avoid my thorn." Don't go there with me!

But here's the thing: when we believe that we have triggers, buttons, and thorns, we're giving away all of our power. We're making others responsible for how we feel. The alternative is to understand you can remove that thorn...and if you *remove* it, you will never have to think about it again.

So how do you know what your thorns are?

Disturbance tells you. Just like pain happens when a physical thorn gets stuck in your skin, disturbance happens when you believe you have a metaphorical thorn. This is why the last chapter's lesson on understanding emotion — and how to feel and identify what emotion you're experiencing — is so important.

If something touches your thorn — let's say your mother says something — and you notice a disturbance, you can then decide what to do about it. To remove the thorn, confront the feeling and ask yourself, "Do I like being disturbed?" The answer is usually "no." Although it can sometimes be "yes" (and I'll explain why with a personal story later on).

This chapter is about understanding where that disturbance actually comes from, and learning how to be aware.

I've been known to get mightily disturbed when my mother sends me emails. I read tone and meaning into everything she writes. Before I knew better, my "thorn" was telling me: she's picking a fight with me, she disrespects me, and she thinks I am stupid. Even though I had gotten to the point where I knew better than reacting in the moment and firing back, I would still become incredibly angry and/or hurt.

The reason is not because of what she actually wrote in the emails, but rather because of what I made it mean (e.g. she's picking a fight, she disrespects me, she thinks I am stupid). Now, of course there is all kinds of history here. More than 50 years of it. But what I didn't realize is that I had a very old, unconscious thought that was running the show: *she's attacking me = I am her victim.*

That was my thorn. Before I learned this distinction, no matter what my mother said or did, I saw it as an attack. I spent a lot of time avoiding, fearing, and being angry. Those emotions tended to drive behavior that I am not proud of.

While I would tell anyone who would listen that I was pissed off or hurt, the fact of the matter is that I also *liked* being angry at my mother. I liked this disturbance because I believed that my anger protected me and my "I am her victim" thorn, just like the woman with the thorn in her arm believed that staying out of the woods protected her. Once I understood that, I was able to start removing my thorn.

Your mother may well be deliberately manipulating you. She may know your buttons well enough to activate your meltdown sequence. When you recognize that this is what she's doing, you can choose not to allow it to work.

One client said to me, "My mother pushes my buttons so hard that I end up in tears every time I talk to her." And boy, could I relate. I used to think my mother liked being able to make me react; she liked having that kind of power over me. And maybe that was true.

So what do you do when you believe your mother is doing this on purpose? Do you call her on it or just change your reaction? As my client said to me after understanding and practicing this concept:

"My mother tries to keep the upper hand in our dialogue by pushing my emotional buttons until I lose control. My composure and my reaction *is* my choice. I can practice how to respond in a safe and strong manner when this happens, until it is no longer a predictable pattern for her, or for me."

So how do you start?

Awareness. Start to notice what your reactions are to everything and everyone around you. In the next chapter, I will show you how to start deactivating your triggers, unbuttoning your buttons, and plucking out those thorns. But for now...

TAKE ACTION:
JUST NOTICE + BECOME THE OBSERVER

Take a week to experiment with noticing and observing (especially in regards to your interactions with your mother or anyone with whom you feel "reactive," past or present). Nothing more.

Instead of engaging in the behaviors of other people, or with every thought you have, just *look*. Pretend you are here only to observe. When you just look but don't engage, it's interesting how you can release yourself from your own stories about what other people are sharing. How you save more energy for you. How it helps still the mind.

You just recognize the trigger ("oh look, there it is"), pause, notice what emotions come up, and choose to be fascinated ("how interesting it is that I now feel xyz emotion as a result") rather than being frustrated and beating yourself up for having the trigger in the first place.

Of course it doesn't mean you go mute in a conversation. If appropriate, you can say, "Oh," or, "I see what you mean," or, "Oh yes I hear what you're saying," or the powerful, "You could be right."

You can also give body cues by looking at others as they speak; nodding your head "yes" that you understand; being still (i.e. not multi-tasking or fidgeting), and giving them your full attention.

When you become the Observer, it's curious how you see people differently. And yourself.

JOURNAL PROMPT:
WHAT ARE YOU NOTICING?

What are you observing? Did you notice your thorns, buttons, and triggers? What are they?

CHAPTER 6

DEACTIVATE YOUR TRIGGERS, UNBUTTON YOUR BUTTONS + PLUCK OUT THOSE THORNS

Remember the email from my mother I told you about in Chapter 4? The one she sent in regards to my grandmother's trust?

I am going to use that example to teach this concept. Here is what went through my head (and came out of my mouth when I shared with a friend), right after I received that email from her:

So this morning, she sent me an email asking if I have to dip into the principal of my grandmother's trust to keep her at the nursing home, or if there are enough dividends generated by her holdings to pay for her care.

I decided to email my contact at the investment house and ask her to help me answer the question. I wanted to have my facts lined up. I didn't hear back from her today, but had planned on responding to my mother when I got the appropriate answer.

This evening, my mother wrote again and asked if I had an answer — or did I have to check with my husband or my grandmother's lawyer. I was pissed. I made it mean that my mother thinks I'm an idiot who couldn't possibly figure this out on her own.

Besides...I don't have to jump when she says jump. Fuck you, mom. *So next, I emailed the lawyer and asked if I am legally obligated to respond to her original question? It's not that I don't want to respond, but I don't want to be manipulated or strong-armed into it.*

Fuck. *I know this is all a big story. And I am* still *looking for permission outside of myself to tell me that I don't have to keep up this charade with this woman! My fucking mother!* Anger. *Yes, I am angry! I've been allowing myself anger from time to time (really truly allowing myself to feel it and express it...not to her...no need to do that), but not enough to cut it off for good, because then the guilt takes over and I think I* should *be evolved enough...I should be able to* manage *my mind enough...to love her even when she fucking pushes my fucking buttons. And then I beat myself up for having the fucking button in the first place.*

I am betting you can relate on some level. Here's how to slow it all down, and start to make sense of all the crap swirling in your head.

Every issue or problem that we encounter can be broken down into five interrelated components, with changes in one component affecting the others. This is the basic structure of human behavior, emotion, and cognition — and it is based on the work of Brooke Castillo, my mentor, Master Coach instructor, and founder of The Life Coach School.

Circumstances are the things that happen in the world around us that we can't control: the weather, our past, and other people's behavior. Circumstances are factual and neutral, without judgment.

Example: *"My mother sent me an email."*

Thoughts are our stories about the circumstances. Thoughts are the opinions and judgments that constantly run through our minds. Sometimes we're aware of them, but often we aren't. We choose (key word) thoughts about the circumstances in our lives.

Examples: *"She's picking a fight with me"* and, *"She thinks I'm stupid,"* and, *"I'm an idiot who couldn't possibly figure this out on my own,"* and, *"I don't have to jump when she says jump."*

We might not be able to change our circumstances, but we can change what we think about those circumstances. We often don't realize it, but each and every thought we have, we choose. It takes effort at first, but we can interrupt our longstanding patterns and create new ones.

Ask yourself, "Why am I choosing to think this thought?" or "What am I making that circumstance mean?"

Our thoughts create our feelings.

Feelings (or emotions) are energy in motion — literal vibrations that we experience in our bodies — and they are directly related to the thoughts we're thinking. Emotions are voluntary because we can change what we feel by changing our thoughts.

Example: *feeling spitting angry because I think my mother thinks I'm stupid.*

Actions refer to behavior, reaction, or inaction, and they're directly related to our feelings.

Examples: *passive/aggressive treatment of my mother, bitching and moaning to my husband, bitching and moaning to my friends, and emailing the lawyer with righteous indignation.* (And, if I am honest, it also includes eating to numb out.)

If we want different actions, we can choose different feelings. I will admit, however, in that moment, I didn't *want* to choose different actions, because I wanted to feel justified and "right."

And finally, Results.

Results are the effects of our actions.

Examples: *not being in the driver's seat of my own life, because I am choosing to live in reaction to my mother — and now having friends who dread my phone calls.*

(And, if I am honest, it also includes being overweight because I was eating to numb out.)

Choosing different *actions* will lead to different *results*.

Our results always provide evidence for, and prove, our thoughts. When we believe what we think, we automatically feel and act as if its true, and then we react in ways that get the results that tend to prove us right. This is why our minds can be so tricky. Of course we believe our experience. But we fail to appreciate that it was not the only possible outcome.

When we take the time to slow it all down and see each component, we become much more aware of the impact our thoughts have on our lives.

This is a good place to introduce the other side of victim consciousness, as Lynne Forrest describes it in her book. Remember the inverted triangle, with the Victim on the bottom and the Persecutor and Rescuer in the "one up" positions? When we step out of victim consciousness, the triangle is righted, and the Victim is transformed into an Observer. The Persecutor becomes the Asserter, and the Rescuer becomes the Nurturer.

"When we stop blaming our unhappiness/happiness on what is happening outside of us and start observing/witnessing life instead, we have tapped into Observer consciousness," Lynne says. She goes on to say that Observers see everything that happens as supporting their journey. When Persecutors modify aggressiveness with self-acceptance, they become diplomatic, assertive, confident, grounded in reality, and not afraid to tell the truth. Rescuers become Nurturers, who focus on taking care of themselves, which then allows them to truly empower others, rather than making others dependent on them.

JOURNAL PROMPT:
SELF-COACHING 101

Choose a recent interaction with your mother and break it down. It doesn't matter where you start. Sometimes it's easier to notice how you feel and put that down first.

Circumstances (other people, the past, the weather…keep it neutral…just the facts):

Thoughts (the sentences that run through your mind… opinions, judgments, stories):

Feelings (one word to describe a vibration in your body):

Actions (behavior, inaction, reaction, how you show up):

Results (the effects of actions, behavior, inaction, reaction):

Once you get used to seeing each component separately, and understand how they are connected, it's tempting to want to *quickly* change your thoughts. And then you realize that it's not always that easy. Something else to consider:

There's no such thing as a "deeply entrenched" thought — and this is good news!

At the heart of what I do with my clients is this very work — showing them the connection between their thoughts, feelings, and actions — especially when it comes to thoughts that they believe are deeply entrenched. You may believe this about your thoughts from childhood, thoughts your mother may have given to you, or maybe you have been taught that it's just part of your makeup. Thoughts like:

I'm not good enough.

Who do I think I am?

I can't take care of myself.

I have to do it all.

I'm too big for my britches.

I don't deserve to have what I want.

What usually happens when we work together is, once the client gets it, they want to start changing their negative thoughts as fast as they can. Why? Because negative thoughts create emotions that don't feel good, and when you don't *feel* good, you don't *do* good.

They say, "Those thoughts are what's holding me back and keeping me stuck. They're what's keeping me from having what I want!"

There's an interesting connection between the *desire* to stop thinking negative thoughts and the *ability* to stop thinking negative thoughts. Here's how it works. You notice yourself feeling like crap and you realize there must be a negative thought rolling around in your brain. If you're anything like me, you see the pattern. Then you go into "change that thought" mode.

But "changing your thoughts" reactively like this is really just another form of resistance, judgment, and avoidance. Because underneath those negative thoughts are other thoughts like, "I shouldn't think that," or, "It's so deeply entrenched," or, "UGH I hate that I have these negative thoughts."

We judge those thoughts and thus ourselves, as "bad." The only truth about a consistent, pernicious* thought is that our brains (which are basically machines) have gotten really good at thinking it. That's it. Our brains love to be efficient and they don't care if those thoughts hurt us. That doesn't make us bad, it's actually quite a feat when you think about it!

So, let me say that again: The only reason you continue to think a negative thought is because your brain has gotten good at it. And that's so good to know, because it also means that your brain can get good at thinking other, more helpful thoughts, just as easily. That thought itself is helpful in dispelling the notion that some thoughts are more deeply entrenched than others, which tends to send the message that they're going to be harder to get rid of.

So rather than resisting, trying to change, judging, or pushing away the thoughts that don't feel good, just notice them. Then ask yourself, "what do I want to believe about myself?" And then just watch when those unwelcome thoughts show up (rather than beating yourself up for having them).

> *"When we TRULY understand that we are punching ourselves in the face, and that it hurts, we don't have to ask what to make our hands do instead, we just stop. And we don't have to remind ourselves not to do it...or to distract ourselves from doing it."*
>
> **BROOKE CASTILLO**

*I LOVE the word "pernicious." It means "having a harmful effect, especially in a gradual or subtle way."

CHAPTER 7

DO NO HARM, BUT TAKE NO SHIT: HOW TO SET EMPOWERED BOUNDARIES

Most women I work with believe that as long as they are not actively engaged with their mothers, they are pretty much okay. It's only when they have to interact with their mothers that they find themselves reacting, seemingly not able to "control" themselves.

I like to use the Superman analogy: We are powerful agents in our own lives, and our mothers are Kryptonite. When we're around them, they seem to steal our power!

So the question becomes: Who do you want to *be* — not only in your relationship to your mother — *but in your life*? How do you want to *feel*? How do you want to *show up*? Do you like *who* you are when you are [fill in the blank]?

On some level, you know your mother isn't going to change (or maybe she will, but you can't count on it). Yet you keep acting as if she will. So you might as well focus on the only things you can change: your own thoughts, feelings, and actions.

Something magical happens when you decide to change *yourself* in relation to your mother. No, it's not like you end up with a fairy tale version of your mother, but you begin to develop profound self trust. You trust yourself to have your own back and with that comes peace. (And sometimes, just loosening your own grip on the story of your relationship with your mother leaves room for *her* to change her patterns, too, but right now we're still focusing on *you*.)

I was afraid to set boundaries with my mother for more than 40 years. It's probably more accurate to say that I didn't realize I needed to set boundaries with her until I was about 40, and *then* I was afraid to do it at first.

It came down to one simple truth: I didn't want to set boundaries with her because I was afraid she'd reject me. I was afraid to stand up for myself and for what I needed and wanted, because I didn't know how to handle her not approving or validating me. I was afraid she'd criticize me for needing what I said I needed, and for wanting what I said I wanted.

Because of my fear, I put up with dysfunctional behavior and sometimes outright abuse from her. Not to mention how I treated *myself*. I spent a lot of time being angry, reactive, and defensive, or numbing myself out with food, shopping, and alcohol.

As I mentioned earlier, things came to an ugly head at the end of 2010. She sent me an email that I deemed beyond-the-beyond. Rather than fighting back, trying to defend or explain myself, I told her never to call or email me again. *I was done.*

Rather than easing my angry, reactive, and defensive feelings, after taking this step I found myself angrier and more defensive, with guilt and deep sadness thrown in for good measure. I spent a lot of time focused on all the ways she'd done me wrong — to help me feel better about cutting her out of my life.

But in reality, I was out of integrity with myself. Since then, it has been my mission to take full responsibility for my life, starting with my own emotions. And a big part of that has meant learning how to set empowered boundaries with my mother (and others).

A lot of times, before we learn how to have healthy boundaries, we believe that our mothers treat us the way they do "because we let them." We think we are supposed to be able to control the way she treats us (probably because that's what's been modeled: our mothers tried to control us in the same way). We contort ourselves trying every conceivable thing in an effort to change, fix, or curtail the challenging aspects of the relationship. Or maybe someone else has suggested that the way your mother behaves is because of something you are doing (or not doing) wrong.

If you've been in therapy, it's probably been suggested to you that you learn how to set boundaries, which is the logical next step when you notice that you can't control the way your mother treats you.

Many of us (and in many cases our mothers) believe that boundaries are about other people's behavior — that they are designed to make other people do what we want them to do (or stop doing what we don't want them to do), in order for us to be happy. That's why so many women struggle with this crucial life skill. It wasn't taught or modeled for them in a realistic way, at least not in the way I am about to explain it.

Setting boundaries *with our mothers* is only one part of the equation, because sometimes our mothers will flatly refuse to respect them. So setting boundaries with *ourselves* in turn commits us, lovingly, to something other than our destructive trigger behaviors as a next step. Knowing we are in integrity with ourselves *and* with our mothers means we are truly keeping our word to ourselves.

First, let's talk about what a good, healthy boundary is not. Healthy boundaries are not:

- Mean, rude, or selfish
- Orders
- Designed to control, manipulate, coerce, or threaten others
- Meant to change someone else's behavior
- Ultimatums

So what is a healthy boundary? A healthy emotional or personal boundary is:

A line you draw around yourself and your own behavior. Like a physical property boundary, it delineates where you end and where others start.

- A tool used to promote self-responsibility and empowerment.

- A gift you give to others and to yourself.

- A meaningful way for you to take care of and protect yourself.

Weak or non-existent boundaries promote enmeshment and emotionally childish behaviors, which distances us from others.

There are two parts to setting a boundary.

The Request: You ask your mother to stop doing something that infringes on your property (literally or emotionally).

The Consequence: You tell her what *you* will do if she doesn't comply with your request. It is an action that *you* will take.

Here are some examples:

Request: Please stop yelling at me.

Consequence: If you don't stop yelling, I am going to leave/hang up the phone/not respond.

Request: Please don't smoke in my house.

Consequence: If you continue to smoke in my house, I will ask you to leave.

Notice that when you make the request, the consequence is the action that you will take. Your mother can behave however she would like. The goal isn't to control her, as much as you might like to do that.

Now, here's the tricky part. Most of us want to have clear boundaries (especially with our mothers), but we don't want to follow through on the consequence part. We don't want to take the action that we say we're going to take. We get even angrier with our mothers if we have to follow through. We believe that she *should* respect and honor our boundaries!

And that is the number one mistake my clients make when setting boundaries with their mothers: *believing that once they set their boundaries, their mothers will respect and not step over them.* It bears mention that your mother didn't teach you to set boundaries. Perhaps she has never been taught to use or respect them, either! And just as it wasn't *your* fault this wasn't taught, it isn't her *fault* she doesn't know what she didn't experience.

It's not your mother's job or responsibility to respect your boundaries...it's yours. It's your job to know what they are, to honor them, and to keep your word to *yourself* if your boundaries are crossed. We have to love and honor ourselves enough to set proper boundaries with our mothers, not just for our sake, but also for theirs.

Setting good, healthy boundaries with my mother was one of the hardest things I've ever done, especially given that there were 40+ years of a pattern in place, my *not* setting boundaries with her. But it was also one of the most empowering things I've ever done. I was finally being honest. And I finally felt in integrity with myself — and with her.

Let me tell you what's amazing about that. I now rarely have any resentment, bitterness, or anger when it comes to my mother. Because I have honored my boundaries, rather than feeling resentful, bitter, or angry, I feel *love*.

Here's an example. My mother smokes. She especially likes to smoke when she's in the car (whether she's driving or someone else is). I prefer not to be exposed to smoke. We used to have quite the passive-aggressive drama around it. I'd seethe with anger and say something like, "Can't you wait??" I would open all the windows and she would close them.

I made it mean that she disrespected me and even wanted to harm my health. She made it mean that I was critical of her and was trying to control her.

I finally decided to try setting a boundary around this when she asked me to drive her somewhere. The day before, I made my request: "Mom, I would appreciate it if you didn't smoke in my car. If you'd like to smoke, I will pull over so you can get out and do just that." She agreed. Another time, when she was the one driving, I suggested: "Mom, if you want to smoke in the car, that's fine, I'll drive separately in my own car."

Notice how my language permitted her to continue to smoke, and I didn't have to get angry or upset or make it mean anything. I didn't try to control her behavior. I just controlled mine. Having good healthy boundaries prevents us from having to accept the consequences of someone else's behavior because we're managing our own instead.

So how does setting healthy boundaries in this fashion empower you? It promotes self-kindness, self-care, and self-responsibility. It puts you back in the driver's seat of your own life, and allows you to reclaim the power you've been giving to your mother. It helps you love and accept her for who she is, allowing her to behave exactly as she wants to, while taking care of yourself by honoring your needs.

Boundaries are designed specifically for physical and emotional self-care, not for getting others to behave a certain way so you can feel better. This is about managing your own business, and never about controlling someone else.

There are a lot of women who don't want to set proper boundaries with their mothers because they're afraid of consequences. They don't want to risk losing the relationship, or they're afraid their mothers will say "no" and will continue to infringe on their personal and emotional space. (That was me for a very long time). They're afraid that if they take care of themselves and tell the truth, they might make their mothers angry (and then not be able to handle it). So in order to not risk this, they don't set boundaries and they stay in a relationship that is based on lies and resentment.

MY BEST BOUNDARY-SETTING TIPS

1. Decide that you value yourself enough to establish boundaries, and that you value your mother enough to teach her how to be with you.

2. Be compassionate. You are modeling an important skill for effective communication. Being compassionate and setting boundaries go together.

3. If you're frustrated, angry, or resentful, you're not ready to set a boundary. Work through those emotions first (and remember that you're not bad for having those emotions). Journal (or talk with someone who WON"T continue to validate your anger) until you can get to a space of calm, peace, and love. The reason you are upset is not because of what your mother is doing (or not doing), it's because you don't have proper boundaries in place, and you haven't been speaking your truth.

4. Once you're clean and clear (which basically means that you've taken responsibility for your upset), then you can have a boundary conversation.

5. Charge neutral. When you are setting a boundary, it is critical that you use a neutral tone of voice. If there is a

negative (or falsely positive) charge to your communication, then the message can get lost and the clarity of the boundary becomes clouded. Practice speaking without a charge in your voice so it feels natural.

6. Practice your new skill with someone who will offer little resistance. Get a feel for what it is like to make the request. When you get more confident, you can start setting boundaries with your mother.

7. Be responsible for your own communication, but understand that you are *not* responsible for how your mother receives or interprets it, nor for how *she* feels as a result. Create clear, direct ways of communicating, and allow your mother to feel how she chooses.

8. Don't take it personally if your mother doesn't change, or if she doesn't respect your boundary. How she chooses to behave, act, and think has nothing to do with you. You can only be responsible for your own communication.

9. Be willing to risk the relationship. When it comes to our mothers, this cuts right to our little-girl cores. But the fact is, we're not little girls any more, and we can survive and thrive without our mother's approval or validation.

> "Outside abuse wanes once we realize that how we are treated by others has a lot to do with how much abuse we will tolerate. Once we come to understand that to accept abusive treatment from others is, in reality, us abusing ourselves. <u>When we fail to define the level of abuse we will tolerate — we inadvertently open ourselves to those who have no defined limits either. Setting healthy boundaries is an inside job. Decide what your own healthy limits need to be, and live as if you have the right to claim them. You may notice that others start treating you like they recognize and respect your limits too!</u>"
>
> **LYNNE FORREST**

TAKE ACTION:
READY TO SET SOME BOUNDARIES?

(Time to get your journal or Peaceful Daughter Workbook...)

Describe the boundary violation. How is your mother infringing on your personal or emotional space?

Get clean and clear. What is your truth? What do you need to take responsibility for?

What is the boundary you'd like to set?

The Request:

The Consequence (what you will do):

What are your fears around establishing this boundary?

What will the benefits of establishing this boundary be?

How will you communicate this boundary?

How will you ensure your boundary is honored?

CHAPTER 8

BUT MOTHERS AREN'T SUPPOSED TO...

One year, just prior to Mother's Day, I saw one of those "things you should never say to..." type articles. It was entitled "13 Things No Estranged Child Needs To Hear On Mother's Day." Of course I read it.

From the list, here's item #9: "Some people don't even have mothers! You'll regret this when she's gone."

I chose this specific article because of the subject, and because it points to a common theme that plays out between mothers and daughters, not to mention other relationships. Our (mostly unconscious) desire to remain in the victim role is rewarded by implying that others shouldn't say certain things to us.

"Don't say these things to me because I might feel bad or mad or sad."

I get it. Sometimes people (including our mothers) say mean, rude, annoying, or thoughtless things. Sometimes they don't know the whole story. And sure, we all wish people would think before they speak.

What if, instead of creating rules for others in regards to what they can or can't say to us, we just let them be who they are and say what they want to say? What if, instead of being offended or outraged, we changed or managed our own thoughts and behavior — rather than scolding, should-ing, or "educating" them?

When I've got my big-girl panties on, I am not "triggered" by what other people say (even my mother!). I am responsible for *myself*. Managing my response means I get to choose to ignore what my mother said, change the subject, or even walk away. She gets to continue saying whatever she wants to say, or doing whatever she wants to do.

I got this concept on a whole 'nother level several years ago when I told a fellow life coach, "My mother stabbed me in the heart with an email," and she said to me, "You stabbed yourself in the heart with what you made her email mean."

I retorted, "But mothers aren't supposed to give their daughters knives with which to stab themselves in the heart!"

Her reply? "Why not?"

Now I know better, but back then I was *soooooo* attached to my story and my role as my mother's victim, that I couldn't see it any other way. This might seem a little harsh, but it brings up a good point: As Byron Katie says, when we argue with what happened, by saying it shouldn't have happened that way, we *create* pain for ourselves.

The point isn't to become a robot who is automatically and immediately immune to what your mother does or says. It's about learning to notice the disturbance and to then ask yourself, "what's really going on here? What am I making it mean?"

It's also about understanding that we can grieve the considerate, nurturing relationship we wish we had. It's not *wrong* that I felt hurt, but letting that hurt *drive my life* was definitely a problem for me (and I will share a recent example of how I didn't let hurt drive my life in Chapter 13).

We have *shoulds* and *shouldn'ts* all over our lives, not just for ourselves, but for everyone else, including (especially?) our mothers. And why not? Your mother most likely has a whole list of *shoulds* and *shouldn'ts* for you, too!

One of the most powerful exercises I ever did, when I decided it was time to go deep in regards to my mother issues, was to make a list of all the things I thought my mother should or shouldn't do (or say), and then acknowledge that the reason I wanted her to change is because of how I thought I would feel. In a word: *happier.*

Most of the women I work with believe they would happier if their mothers changed or behaved differently. I have come to understand that what my mother says or does has no impact on me emotionally until I think about it, interpret it, and *choose to make it mean something*. I was really good at making what she said and did mean something *bad*, which in turn made me sad and angry.

I believed that if she just said and did what I wanted her to, then I could be happy. And I'll tell you something right now: all the shoulds and shouldn'ts I had for my mother guaranteed one thing only, more emotional pain. Having these conditions put my emotions in my mother's hands, and if she didn't abide by my list, I was guaranteed to feel negative emotions. Then I blamed her because I felt bad.

Because I gave control of my emotions to my mother, I perpetuated my hidden belief that I am powerless and that I couldn't take care of myself. When I finally took responsibility for my emotions, I got to feel and experience what I wanted on my own terms, no matter what she did or didn't do (or say).

This doesn't mean it's *bad* to want your mother to do certain things, or to *ask* her for something you want. Just understand that you will create pain for yourself if you expect her to meet your needs or make you feel good. That's *your* job.

It's also equally important to remember that you are not responsible for *her* emotions and that your mother is in charge of how *she* interprets your behaviors. When you let her off the hook for how you feel, you *also* will give yourself permission to let yourself off the hook for how she feels.

Can you see how having an unwritten list of shoulds and shouldn'ts for your mother is different from having healthy boundaries?

Time to take out your journal (or your Peaceful Daughter Workbook)...

JOURNAL PROMPTS:
CHANGING BEHAVIORS

Write, in detail, what you think your mother should do... what you'd like her to do.

For each item, write down why you want her to behave this way.

How would you feel differently if she behaved this way?

How would your thoughts about her change if she behaved in this way?

Do you want her to behave this way even if she doesn't want to? Why or why not?

What do you make it mean that she doesn't behave this way?

When she wants you to behave a certain way so she can feel good, what is that like for you?

In what other ways has she made you responsible for her feelings?

How might you let yourself off the hook for her feelings? And how might you do the same for her?

CHAPTER 9

MOTHER AS A VERB, NOT A NOUN

The bulk of this chapter comes from the teachings of Martha Beck.

Martha tells a story about a Zen monk who was waiting to greet the emperor of Japan. Just before the emperor arrived, he turned to a fellow monk and said, "I'll be back later."

"Later" turned out to be 12 years later. When his peers asked where he'd been and why he'd left, he explained, "As I waited for the emperor, I felt my palms begin to sweat. I knew that I was attached to social roles because my body was tense. I've been meditating to lose that attachment. I came back as soon as I could."

Martha says that in our culture, we often think that detaching from something means that we are less devoted to it, or that we love it less. The monk's story comes from the opposite perspective. When we are attached to people's roles, we cannot see them from a place of simple compassion.

Your mother will always be your mother, but it's time to detach yourself, not only from her role, but also from her beliefs.

From the time you were born, and even before that, your relationship with your mother served as the bedrock and template for your relationship with yourself. Your mother's beliefs were the basis for your own. You learned to treat yourself the way your mother treated herself, and the way she treated you. This is generally a completely unconscious process. You internalize what you experience.

The nature of the mother-daughter relationship is such that it seems to be etched in stone — permanent and unchangeable. Thus, it often feels like your relationship with yourself is the same.

Remember back in Chapter 3 when I said many of my clients are women who have an underlying "I'm not good enough," or a, "Something is wrong with me" story? You have come to see that this was true of me, as well.

And those stories — those beliefs — have played out in my own life in myriad ways, from believing that I wasn't worthy of being loved by a good man (and thus I ended up first married to a guy from Brazil who just needed a green card) to binge eating and spending more money than I had.

As a result, I spent many, many years believing that I couldn't take care of myself. It wasn't until I started practicing acceptance (i.e., not arguing with reality) that I realized I didn't have to believe my mother's stories, nor did I have to blame her for my having adopted them. I simply needed to learn and do differently. And as an adult, this was my choice.

I'd also heard plenty about learning to "mother" myself, but it seemed like such a foreign concept. I thought it meant blaming myself and being super "strict" with myself, such that it would be unpleasant, hard, and involve suffering! This is pretty much the way I was raised, so of course I didn't have anything to which to compare it.

Through years of trial and error, here's what I have learned about my mothering myself: It's the ultimate in self-care. Self-care isn't just about bubble baths and pedicures, it's the deliberate practice of acknowledging, honoring, and meeting my own needs (as I define them), or making sure that my needs get met. Meaning, it's all my responsibility. And it requires no force, willpower, or bargaining with myself.

So what does it look like? Rather than blaming your mother, or yourself, for all the things that you think are "wrong" with you, you can start to change your internal definitions of what it *means* to be mothered. In turn, you stop looking to an imperfect human female (your mother) for perfect parenting.

Martha Beck says you are being mothered when anyone (including yourself) offers you acceptance, nourishment, instruction, or empowerment.

Acceptance: "Mothering starts with unconditional love without demands or expectations." In other words, you don't have to change in order to be loved. Is there someone in your life who loves you in this way? For me, it's my husband, who has an incredibly strong maternal instinct for a man.

Nourishment: "Sustenance, comfort and care, whether physical or emotional, are components of motherhood. Anyone who nurtures you, in mind, body, or heart is mothering you." This is something that I have learned to do for myself, quite well.

Instruction: "Mothers teach constantly, showing both by example and by explanation, what their children must know in order to live well." Who do you choose as your teachers?

Empowerment: "Mothers are intent on working themselves out of a job, by building in those they mother the courage and confidence to become independent."

Once you've detached your concept of motherhood from a particular human being, you can be open to receiving mothering from a variety of sources, including yourself. In which areas could you use more mothering? Martha suggests completing these sentences (these are included in your Peaceful Daughter Workbook):

I feel useless, unlovable, and disgusting when:

I feel empty and needy when:

I feel stupid and ignorant when:

I feel helpless and incapable when:

By being honest and open to seeing connections to current circumstances, you will see the areas in which you need "to find the kind of maternal love that can nurture your unmet needs."

Feelings of uselessness, disgust, stupidity, and helplessness stem from thoughts you are having about yourself. And while I highly recommend uncovering and identifying those thoughts (using the Journal Prompt in Chapter 6), so you can meet your own needs — it can also be helpful to commit to finding other people who can offer you acceptance, nourishment, instruction, and empowerment in those areas. This may be a reciprocal relationship, or you may be open to receive from some people and perhaps offer to others.

If it's your mother, great, ask her. But if she can't or won't provide it, open yourself to finding someone who can.

Good mothering is available to you if you are willing to let go of expectations that will never be met, and open to see what is being offered to you in this moment. Martha says that although all mothers are limited, the force of motherhood is not. It surrounds you every day, in all sorts of guises, some predictable and ordinary, some startling and extraordinary.

When you do this, you start to shift away from seeing your mother as limited. You shift from blaming her, to finding your unconditionally loving inner mother. Just like you have an inner child, you can also learn to develop an inner mother. Your inner mother is your adult self, with all your knowledge and power, supported by higher forces, including your own prefrontal cortex.

This happens as you begin to see the reality of your own lovableness, goodness and value, no matter what's happening out there — no matter what your mother is or isn't doing. You are no longer relying on her for validation or approval.

You are better able to receive love from others because you are no longer invested in seeing yourself as *less than* in order to be loyal to your mother, and because you are not waiting for her to show up the way *you* needed or wanted her to.

You are able to see your whole self with compassionate objectivity, which means you acknowledge the faults, flaws, mistakes, while also acknowledging your goodness and value. External approval may come, but you no longer need it to *feel okay*. Some additional questions to ask yourself:

Where do I need to love myself more?

What am I here to learn?

What is it that I believe about myself that this situation is showing me?

What can I do about it?

If there's one thing I want you to do most of all, it's to approach yourself and this process with an attitude of curiosity, fascination, kindness, and compassion. All it requires is a willingness to practice and to understand that just like a little baby learning to walk, you will fall down, and you will want to get right back up and try again. After all, it's exciting, and you desire to see where you might go!

You can become the mother you always wanted for yourself. And you can create a relationship with your mother from a place of unconditional love and empowerment, even if she is no longer here or if you choose not to communicate with her at this time.

As I said in Chapter 3, part of mothering yourself is learning to retell your story in a way that supports your growth. Below are some journal prompts that will help you redefine who you are now, what you believe, and what you want to believe.

Journal or Peaceful Daughter Workbook time!

JOURNAL PROMPTS:
WHAT I BELIEVE

Your mother was your first teacher. What beliefs, values, and lessons did she teach directly (by telling you) and indirectly (via modeling)? This can be a list of things you cherish or things you wish you didn't learn. Or better, both!

What did you learn about your body? About food? About your sexuality? About men? About other women? About marriage? About money? About friendship?

What do *you* believe and value? Are they the same as what your mother taught? What do you want to believe and value?

What agreements (usually silent) have you made with your mother without realizing it? Agreements like: "I won't shine too brightly because I am afraid she'll feel threatened."

Where did your mother fall short? What didn't you receive that you needed and/or wanted? How can you start to acknowledge, honor, and meet your own needs (or get them met)?

In what areas of your life are you not kind and gentle with yourself? How can you demonstrate to yourself (and thus, your own children, if you have them) that you matter?

What are the consistent, negative thoughts running through your mind? Are they your own thoughts or are they your mother's? Consider that those thoughts contribute to negative emotions, which drive negative behavior.

And finally, remember that it's what you model that makes more of an impact on your children, rather than what you say. What are you modeling?

CHAPTER 10:

WHEN YOU DECIDE TO CHANGE

The process of choosing to wake up and change wasn't easy on me, or on my mother. As of this writing, our relationship consists only of emails sent back and forth in regards to my grandmother (her mother) for whom I am legal guardian.

After several years of no contact, we began a shaky back and forth via email. It was an excellent opportunity for me to practice the concepts I've outlined in this book. We got together in person during the summer of 2014. The visit had its good moments, as well as some tense ones, as I chose to maintain my boundaries. There were some conversations I wasn't willing to have, and I let her know that those subjects were none of my business.

Additionally, I explained to her that I no longer needed or wanted her approval, I was no longer making her responsible for my feelings, and I was also not taking responsibility for hers. I said, "If you want to feel disappointed or ashamed of me, that's on you."

When we said our goodbyes, she asked, "Does this mean we can call each other and see each other again?" I said, "Of course."

That didn't happen, although we continued to communicate via email. A few months before this book was published actually I asked if she'd like to get together again. Her response indicated that she didn't see the point in it, and further, that she felt uncomfortable being around me.

It stung. I cried. Hard, heaving, can't-catch-my-breath sobs. The little girl in me felt rejected by her mommy. I immediately wanted to call/email/post on social media to anyone who would listen and say...

"See??! Look what's she's done to me now!!"

I was creating a reason to have my "story" playing (un)happily in the background again, rather than creating a new one. The adult me, however, felt relieved. And then guilty, because I was relieved in part — and also because, deep down inside, I *wanted* her to reject me so I wouldn't have to be the bad guy. I also observed it provided the opportunity for a massive pity-party!

So perhaps part of me kind of *wanted* something like this to happen, so I could continue to be "right" about her. Yet a part of me was feeling guilty for having "abandoned" my mother when I had become more emotionally grounded and mature. Maybe I created this dynamic so she would reject or punish me? Or maybe I was just putting the ball in her court, allowing her to be the one to choose the engagement between the two of us? It was easy to think myself into a circle around all of this.

Within the space of about an hour (rather than days, weeks, months...years), I went from pity-me-mode (helpless little girl who can't take care of herself), into fuck-you-mode (channeling my inner rebellious teenager), and into pretend-evolved-adult-mode ("I am so above this"), and right back to pity again.

That's when I caught myself in the middle of my own damned pattern and actually laughed out loud. Thanks to my mother, I got to see just how good my mind has gotten at going for the pity. I could practically feel the neurons firing down the well-worn pathways in my brain. My brain *likes* pity.

And so I asked myself, "Who do I want to be in this moment? What can I say that will allow me to like myself?" My answer: I want to be a non-reactive, non-defensive, non-pity-seeking grown-ass woman who chooses to love her mother without indulging in the drama. *I want to be free.*

So I hit reply and wrote, "Okay, let me know if you change your mind."

I am free.

I think it's important to say that when you change the parameters of the way you behave in your relationship with your mother, your mother might not like it, she may fight it to some degree, or be puzzled by it. There will be some wobbly tension while new boundaries and patterns are put into place. This is a very, very common experience, and many coaches have names for it.

My message to you is this: While you can't control your mother, or how she might react to you choosing to change, you can choose to be *okay*. That's not a guarantee that you will never be sad or angry again, but rather that you will *have your own back*. You will know how to handle whatever emotions arise as you navigate your relationship with your mother and yourself. Knowing that you get to choose how you want to feel is the most empowering aspect of this process because it puts you in the driver's seat of your life.

CHAPTER 11:

CHOOSING TO LOVE YOUR MOTHER UNCONDITIONALLY, AS THE GREATEST GIFT YOU CAN GIVE YOURSELF

(A HOW-TO GUIDE)

So now that you understand the nature of your thoughts and emotions, and how they are connected, let me ask you this: How do you want to feel about your mother? Of all the feelings that are available to you, what might you choose?

One day, a couple of years ago, Brooke Castillo suggested to me that choosing love, *unconditional* love even, feels the best, knowing that when we feel great, the actions we take and the ways we behave help us have the kind of results we want in our lives.

At first, I thought it was *unlikely* that I could ever love my mother unconditionally, not to mention *dangerous*. As I've said, I spent *years* feeling chronic anger, bitterness, and resentment towards my mother. Although I knew it wasn't good for me, I believed that those emotions *protected* me.

I was afraid that if I let those feelings of hurt go, she would "win" — and I would end up giving in to whatever she wanted and would always have to agree with her, which meant that I'd never escape from her abusive or dysfunctional behavior. I wanted to love her, but I didn't know how to do that and preserve myself at the same time.

For me, back then, it was an either/or proposition: either I stay angry and protect myself, or I love her and let her swallow me whole (at least that's what it felt like would happen). That's because I didn't understand that unconditional love is an emotion that I get to *choose* to feel — not a concept, action, or behavior that is *forced* on me or even *expected* of me.

All emotions — from fear and anger to joy and love — are nothing more and nothing less than vibrations that we feel in our bodies. Shame usually comes with a hot, prickly feeling around my face and neck. Grief is an exquisite ache in my throat and heart. Anger feels like the wind has been knocked out of me (and it's heavy too), and I feel slightly choked. Anxiety is weak knees and a shakiness in my belly (sometimes I actually shiver).

And love? It's a heart-melting, warm sensation in my chest and belly. The more I understand about love, the more I know that it's not an emotion that comes with conditions. I can create it and feel it because I simply want to.

And because I like the way unconditional love feels, I made a conscious choice to feel it for my mother, rather than choosing anger, bitterness, and resentment (which don't feel so great). When you choose to feel love, you get to feel love, without conditions.

Now that I've learned how to notice what I'm feeling, and how to connect those feelings to the thoughts I am thinking, rather than attaching it to what she says or does, I get to choose. What has most helped me love my mother is understanding that she doesn't have to change in order for me to feel it. There are no conditions. It's my responsibility, not hers. I don't have to rely on her to do anything in order for me to feel it. As a result of choosing to feel unconditional love for my mother, I understand that — as imperfect as we both are — she was (and still is) the perfect mother for me, and I am the perfect daughter for her. I can now embrace the qualities in me that are also in her, whether I like them or not.

I've also established boundaries that come from a place of love and respect for both of us. And most importantly, when I let her off the hook for being responsible for my feelings, I also let myself off the hook for being responsible for hers. We are two autonomous women. A mother and a daughter. Powerful in our own separate rights.

Most people equate unconditional love with unconditionally tolerating bad behavior. Here's what I ask you to consider: *Love is always an available choice.* You don't always have to make it, but you always have the choice.

Love doesn't know the difference between conditional and unconditional. Loving unconditionally does not mean tolerating bad behavior or not having boundaries — in fact, I'd say good boundaries are part of what allows love to thrive.

If you'd like to cultivate more unconditional love in your life in general, here are some simple steps you can take:

Close your eyes and take a deep breath. Unlock those shoulders. Soften your eyes. Take another deep breath.

1. Think about someone or something that you love. Think of how much happiness this person or thing brings to your life and how much you love them.

2. Continue focusing on this person or thing until you start to feel a physical sensation. Describe it. Where in your body do you feel it? Does it have a texture? A temperature? A color?

3. Now think about someone for whom it's hard to feel love. Summon up any anger, resentment, and bitterness you have towards this person until you start to feel it physically. Get to know it just like you got to know what unconditional love feels like. Which feels better?

4. Understand that choosing to feel unconditional love is a favor you do for yourself. It's available to you right now if you want it.

5. Understand that loving unconditionally does not mean tolerating bad behavior from others, or even having to see or speak to someone. It just means that when you think of this person, you choose to still feel amazing.

CHAPTER 12:

WHAT'S ON THE OTHER SIDE OF THE STRUGGLE?

> "I have nothing to prove. I have nothing to hide. I have nothing to defend. I have nothing to protect.
>
> I am free."
>
> **LISA NICHOLS**

> "Each of us creates solely out of a clear mind, a free-flowing mind, creativity just flowing nonstop. We don't need pain to be creative. In fact, it's limiting. If you look at yourself during times that you've done things that you've absolutely loved, you haven't been suffering. You were free."
>
> **BYRON KATIE**

I don't remember a time that I didn't struggle, on some level, in my relationship with my mother. Throughout this book I have shared some examples. One of my earliest memories is of me sitting in my high chair, crying with rage and shock, because she'd dumped a bowl of cereal and milk over my head — apparently because I was being stubborn and wouldn't finish it. A more recent memory: The time I smiled at her through an open window, and she sneered and gave me the finger (yes that one).

Hopelessness. Helplessness. Anxiety. Self-loathing. Impotent rage. Blame and shame. Oh the blame and the shame. Blaming myself, blaming my mother. Being ashamed for blaming. 'Round and 'round it went.

As you now know, intense emotions can lead you to do some pretty dramatic things. For me, it was binge eating, looking for love in all the wrong places, spending money I didn't have until I was significantly in debt and had to declare bankruptcy, trying to control others to the point where I nearly damaged important relationships, and, at times, lashing out at the people I love.

And on a more subtle, but certainly profound level, I held myself back from fully exploring, using, and sharing my gifts and talents. Wondering who and what I could have been, *if only*, or believing that so much of my time had been wasted "asleep at the wheel" of my life. Lamenting, but not believing it could be otherwise. And then, in a misguided effort to *not* struggle in my relationship with my mother, I cut her out of my life and actually found myself giving it *more* of my time, attention, and energy.

And I can tell you right now, it didn't feel good…not deep down inside where it matters. Even though I was telling myself otherwise, I was not free. I was not at peace.

(I'll say it again, because it's important: For some daughters, the very best, most freeing, peaceful thing to do might actually be to sever ties with their mothers.)

But I knew I needed and wanted something more for myself. It was time to heal on a deeper level (those of you who read my *first* book know that my first conscious healing journey concerned finding peace with food and my body). Many of the same tools that served me then have served me as I do this deeper healing.

And so I did the work on this issue, too (and I will continue to do it, because it is ongoing, for all of us). I asked myself the hard questions, and more importantly, I answered them. And the answers have been profoundly satisfying. For the first time in my life, I know what it's like to…

…live my life without the constant negative thoughts about my mother

…live without thinking that she should approve of my life

…show up in the world as myself and not "in reaction" to her

…be unafraid of her

And although my mother and I have been estranged at times, I didn't have to wait for her to *die* to feel differently. More than one woman has told me that it wasn't until her mother died that she finally felt free. Knowing what I know now, I see that feeling free is not dependent on my mother dying. It isn't dependent on anyone or anything other than myself. True freedom comes from your mind. No one can set you free...only you have the power to do that.

So, somewhere along the line, I decided that I was going to set myself free — whether my mother is alive, whether my mother approves, or not. So what does it look like to feel free?

Imagine not holding yourself back from creating what you want (because you're afraid of what your mother will say)

Imagine being able to say "no" without apology or explanation.

Imagine being able to set empowered boundaries that serve you and strengthen the relationships that mean the most to you.

Imagine taking good care of your physical, mental, spiritual, and emotional self.

Imagine being able to meet your own needs and being able to ask for help in doing so.

Imagine not sabotaging your efforts.

Imagine that you don't have to force yourself.

Imagine that you don't hurt yourself.

Imagine setting goals from a place of excitement, without them being attached to what others think.

Imagine being able to ask yourself how you want to show up in the world, knowing that it's always your choice, and then *doing it*.

Imagine that you aren't afraid to share yourself and your work (sure you might be nervous, but you can handle it).

Imagine not being afraid to "go there" and understanding that "going there" isn't as painful and scary as NOT "going there."

Imagine being able to make mistakes and fail without spiraling into shame and hopelessness.

Imagine being able to have doubts and confusion, knowing it's temporary, even though it sucks in the moment.

Imagine that you have your own sweet back.

Imagine loving your amazing, foolish self.

> *"I must learn to love the fool in me — the one who feels too much, talks too much, takes too many chances, wins sometimes and loses often, lacks self-control, loves and hates, hurts and gets hurt, promises and breaks promises, laughs and cries. It alone protects me against that utterly self-controlled, masterful tyrant whom I also harbor and who would rob me of human aliveness, humility, and dignity but for my fool."*
>
> **THEODORE RUBIN**

CHAPTER 13:

HOW DOES THIS BOOK END?

So here we are, at the end of the book. You are not exactly the same woman you were when you started reading!

What has changed? What is your new reality? What is your new story? How are you empowered? What boundaries have you set? What promises have you made to yourself? What promises have you kept?

Where have you stopped "shoulding" when it comes to yourself and your mother? How have you started taking care of yourself and meeting your own needs? Are you practicing freedom and autonomy? Where do you need to practice more?

You may feel a bit nervous and adrift, wondering if you can really do this on your own. My wish for you is, no matter how you choose to do it, that you make yourself a priority and do this work for you, *not* for your mother. What I know for sure is that the awareness you cultivate is priceless.

Recently someone said to me, "When you can stand on your story, and not let your story stand on you, you'll be able to truly help others." She asked me to tell her the story I now stand on. She also asked me to tell her my "why," e.g.

why I am so passionate about helping women transform their mother stories. Here's what I told her:

The world needs women who are truly impressed with themselves and who are excited to create (and I don't mean in an artistic way, unless that's the way their creativity manifests itself). When women are impressed with themselves, they do amazing things in the world.

They are amazing (not perfect) friends, partners, wives, mothers, sisters. They are confident (not cocky or conceited), and they strive to make a difference, not from a place of desperation or needing to prove something, but from a place of pure joy and aliveness.

When women are impressed with themselves, they are amazing scientists, teachers, dancers, writers, engineers, poets, and business people.

When women are impressed with themselves, they are happy in their own skin. They take excellent care of themselves and are thus able to nurture others.

When women are impressed with themselves, whatever they want to do is okay.

But because of patterns and stories that get passed down, mother to daughter (especially in a dysfunctional patriarchal culture), some women are afraid to be impressed with themselves — and they are afraid to create, afraid to shine, afraid to put themselves first. This is sometimes referred to as the "mother wound." I prefer not to use that language.

I had a mutually abusive, toxic, enmeshed relationship with my mother. As a result of that, I told myself a whopper of a story about me, a story that stood on me for years. That story went something like this: *I am pathetic. I am bad. I am unworthy. I can't trust myself. I can't take care of myself. I should be ashamed of myself.*

Because of that story, and how I felt about that story, I was miserable, reactive, resistant, and scared. I was an underachiever. I was a binge eater, and as I got older, I started sleeping around thinking it was the only way to get a man to love me. I even married a guy so he could get a green card. I spent way more money than I made and ended up declaring bankruptcy. I lashed out at people I loved.

My life wasn't a complete disaster, but I was asleep at the wheel, and I had no idea what was possible for me. I didn't know what I wanted. I didn't know how to desire something for myself.

Having goals and "being responsible" scared me. My anxiety went through the roof. (Funnily enough, it manifested in a severe fear of *other people throwing up*. It almost paralyzed me, especially in the winter months. There were times when I thought I'd become one of those people who couldn't leave her home.) This lasted for years. It's only been recently that I've started to understand that I had some PTSD going on, at the time, as well.

Through various therapies (traditional and not-so-traditional), not to mention reading books about narcissistic mothers and mothers who can't love, I started to wake up. And while the therapy and the books explained a lot, and helped me feel that I was not alone, they also provided an excuse. The story that stood on me turned into this: *Because my mother was and is the way she is, I'm screwed. It's too late for me. I am damaged and that's just the way life happened.*

I was most definitely not impressed with myself.

Sure, from time to time I would experience the real, powerful essence of myself, but the stories I'd been telling myself felt permanent and more potent, plus they were familiar. More than anything else, I unconsciously feared that if I was my real self, my mother wouldn't approve of or love me. I certainly had proof of that...and man, if your mother doesn't love you unless you contort yourself to her desires, who will?

Through a combination of Emotional Freedom Technique (aka "tapping"), writing, and powerful coaching, over the course of a couple of years I disentangled myself from my mother and from the stories I was telling myself about myself and her. I've come home to myself as a powerful, autonomous woman who understands the nature of true creativity.

Relationships that are important to me (with my husband, my stepchildren, my sister, and my friends) have become healthier and stronger. Why? Because what I used to think of as the "truth" about myself isn't true and so I no longer act as if it is.

And best of all, I am impressed with the one person who matters most: *myself.*

I'd be lying if I said that I am done, that I have reached the finish line. When it comes to me and my mother, I will never be done. Now, rather than dread that fact, I relish it. The key to maintaining clarity is continuing to practice the tools.

I am now on a mission to help other women impress themselves by helping them take a close look at their very first relationships: the ones they have with their mothers. For some, perhaps it's a matter of establishing some empowered boundaries, and for others it could go a lot deeper. Some, like me, may decide that having no contact with their mothers is necessary at some point, but with the understanding that you can't delete the relationship.

Or maybe you can redefine and renegotiate a healthier adult relationship with your mother, once you are able to deactivate your triggers and not let your story stand on you. Perhaps your mother would be interested in doing some of this work, too! Wherever you are on the spectrum is the right place for you to be. And right for your mother, when you extend the thinking.

My ideal client is a woman who has been through the therapy and has read the books, who is done looking back with dread, and who wants to look forward, focus on what's possible for her, and have fun while doing it!

Maybe that's you!

I invite you to have a conversation with me (http://www.kclanderson.com/free-session/). During this complimentary "Mother Of All Breakthroughs" calls we will:

1) Discover what is unconsciously blocking you from moving forward with the peace you desire

2) Consider steps you can take to create more peace in your relationship

3) Discuss how you can step into Peaceful Daughter programs that will support you

At the very least, I encourage you stay in touch. The best way to do that is to "like" my Peaceful Daughter Facebook page: https://www.facebook.com/peacefuldaughter

THE PEACEFUL DAUGHTER MANIFESTO

One of the most insidious things adult daughters do is beat themselves up for not having a "great" relationship with their mothers (even if they are no longer alive). I put the word "great" in quotation marks because what "great" means to you, me, or the next woman might be different, but for the sake of this conversation, let's say it looks like this:

Mom and daughter are close, warm, and supportive of each other. Daughter is able to lean on Mom. Mom loves daughter unconditionally. Daughter lovingly helps Mom out when she needs it. They have separate lives, but make it a point to get away together for "girl time," to bond and strengthen their relationship. Daughter adores Mom and tells her friends how lucky she is to have her. Mom is proud of daughter and praises her to all her friends. They genuinely respect each other.

And if it doesn't look like that (or whatever your version of "great" is), then it's your fault, and as a result, you have a constant, low-level feeling of guilt because you haven't been able to fix it by now.

I am here to witness you, represent you, and tell you:

That's not the truth.

There is nothing wrong with you.

It's not your fault.

You are not to blame.

You're not alone, and you don't have to suffer alone, in silence.

All mothers are not loving and buying into the idea that they are (so it must be your fault) only isolates you.

You don't have to live the rest of your life feeling guilty.

There is no such thing as a perfect mother-daughter relationship.

No matter what Hallmark says.

No matter what you see on Facebook.

No matter what "they" say you "should" think/feel/do.

Mothers do not automatically and instinctually love their daughters unconditionally (no matter how our culture portrays them) and it's not taboo to acknowledge that.

Please do not shame or guilt yourself.

It's not on you.

I am taking this stand for you.

What's NOT okay (for me personally, although some of it may be true for you, too):

It's not okay for me to:

Believe it's my responsibility to fix my relationship with my mother (which isn't to say that I've slammed the door shut on our relationship).

Live my life for my mother.

Stop expressing myself because she has told me she doesn't like it when I do.

Place any "shoulds" on my mother.

Expect my mother to change.

Blame myself (or her) for what has happened in the past (although it is okay to acknowledge it).

Hide my light because I'm afraid she might feel threatened by it.

Choose to feel "less than" because of what my mother has said or done.

Beat myself up, emotionally or otherwise.

Binge eat, binge drink, binge shop, or binge-anything-else because of the pain I feel when I chose to beat myself up.

Be boundary-less.

Continue to think I am a victim and she is a villain.

Think of her as a victim and myself as a villain.

Think that either one of us need to be rescued.

It's not okay for me to be anything less than the powerful, peaceful, loving woman I know myself to be.

AN OPEN LETTER TO YOUR MOTHER

Dear [insert your name here]'s mother:

I'm betting that when your daughter talks about the strained relationship she has with you, you interpret it to mean that she thinks you are a bad mother, maybe even a bad person, and that she's one who has suffered, as a result. You might even make it mean that she thinks she's the "good one" in the relationship.

Here's the thing: she's just different.

Because she needed and wanted your love and approval her whole life, she sometimes contorted, changed, and hid herself. She did this not because she thought what she was doing was bad or wrong (because it wasn't) — she did it because she was afraid that if you knew the real her, you would withdraw your love.

And now that she's being her true self, it seems like she's changed! She's not as pliable and malleable. She's not as easily manipulated, and it's caused some friction, or maybe even estrangement.

Here's what you need to know about your daughter: she needs and wants to feel good about herself and her life, but she didn't have the self-discipline to do that when she was enmeshed with you.

Because you were so big and so important to her, she gave you an inordinate amount of her attention. And in so doing, without meaning to, you trained her to separate herself from herself. She loved you so much and stayed enmeshed with you a long time because she thought she might be able to find herself anyway. But as it turned out, she couldn't.

She couldn't not be herself (for you) and be herself (for herself) at the same time.

So she figured, at a minimum, that she needed space because of her lack of self-discipline. She needed space so she could retrain herself back into alignment with who she is...and who she wants to be.

She loves her life. She feels good about herself. She likes to wake up every day and feel alive and on purpose. She wants to talk about happy things and she wants to see the best in others. She wants to feel good about what she gives her attention to. And for a while, when she was with you, she was able to do that. But the longer the two of you were together and the more enmeshed the two of you became, the less able she was to do that. It became a struggle and the struggle sucked the life out of her.

So here's the plan. She is going to choose to feel fabulous. And she is going to do everything in her power to envision you feeling fabulous, too. She could write pages and pages about all the things she loves about you, but she is NOT responsible for how you feel...and you've tried to make her responsible for that every damned day. That's not her job, it's yours.

Her promise to you is that she will be as happy as she can and will never hold you responsible for the way she feels.

(The gist of this letter is based on the work of Abraham-Hicks)

RECOMMENDED RESOURCES

Here are some suggestions for further exploration...some of which are mentioned in the book and some of which are not:

Mother-Daughter Wisdom
BY DR. CHRISTIANE NORTHRUP
http://www.drnorthrup.com

Mindset
BY CAROL DWECK
http://mindsetonline.com

Beyond Victim Consciousness
BY LYNNE FORREST
http://www.lynneforrest.com

The Dark Side Of The Light Chasers
BY DEBBIE FORD
http://debbieford.com

The Language of Emotions
BY KARLA MCLAREN
http://karlamclaren.com

Nonviolent Communication: A Language Of Life
BY MARSHALL B. ROSENBERG
http://www.nonviolentcommunication.com/index.htm

Brooke Castillo
THE LIFE COACH SCHOOL
http://thelifecoachschool.com

Iyanla Vanzant
http://iyanla.com

Martha Beck
http://marthabeck.com

Byron Katie
http://thework.com

Brené Brown
http://brenebrown.com

ACKNOWLEDGEMENTS

Mama Jo Pillmore, friend and mentor, who came into my life so seemingly randomly. Ha! Thank you Mama Jo!

C.J. Blaquera, fellow Life Coach School coach, who asked me that pivotal question: *"Why not?"* Thank you C.J.!

(Lani, Wendi, Grace, Joely, Claire, Talyaa) AND (Liz, Kat, Tara, and Jeanne), who provided a safe place for me to land, and who let me provide them with the same safe place. Thank you ladies!

Brooke Castillo, master coach instructor and founder of The Life Coach School, who held the space for me to do the deepest work I've ever done. Thank you Brooke!

Christie M. Inge, friend and fellow coach, who was instrumental in showing me there might be a different way to deal with my shit. Thank you Christie!

Angela Lauria, Kate Makled, and the rest of The Difference Press team, who lovingly guided me through the writing of this book. Thank you Angela, Kate, and team!

Cynthia and Dorothy, whom I have no doubt were and will continue to be the perfect mother and grandmother for me. Thank you, Mommy and Grandma, for the life lessons, the struggle, the laughs, the tears, all of it.

Tim, husband extraordinaire, there are no words to describe the depth of appreciation and gratitude I feel for you. Thank you dear Timote.

ABOUT THE AUTHOR

Karen C.L. Anderson is a master-certified life coach, author, and blogger who makes sure adult daughters know how to create autonomy, resilience, and empowerment in their lives by helping them redefine who they are in relationship to their mothers.

The sum of her experiences, her wisdom, her innate abilities, and the stuff she's learned along the way, are enough.

But in case you're wondering, Karen has some formal training and she's done lots of hard (the good kind of "hard") work (the motivating, inspirational kind) in order to put some structure around her wisdom and experience:

- She is a Master Certified Coach through the Life Coach School

- She is an Emotional Freedom Techniques practitioner and has completed EFT Training For Trauma, Levels I + II

- She has a Bachelor of Arts degree in Communications from Marist College

She is the author of *AFTER (the before + after): A Real Life Story of Weight Loss, Weight Gain, and Weightlessness Through Total Acceptance*, which was based on her blog, "Before & After: A Real Life Story."

That blog was selected by the Institute for the Psychology of Eating as one of the Top 50 Emotional Eating blogs, and by Shape magazine one of the Top 20 Inspiring Weight Loss Blogs (in 2011).

Prior to all of that? She spent seven years as a freelance writer and before that she spent 17 years trying to fit her right-brained self into a left-brained career as a trade magazine journalist in the field of plastics (and if she had a dime for every time someone mentioned that line from *The Graduate*...).

Most importantly, she's been there and done that.

Karen is married to the love of her life, Tim Anderson (a left-brained engineer), and they live in New London, CT, with their two cats, Bella and Starla. Karen is child-free by choice, has three step kids, and now gets to be Booboo to her stepdaughter's two children.

THANK YOU

Thank you for reading *The Peaceful Daughter's Guide To Separating From A Difficult Mother*! As I token of my gratitude, and to continue the journey we started together, I'd like to offer you a free 1-hour "Mother Of All Breakthroughs" Call.

http://www.kclanderson.com/free-session/

Download your free Peaceful Daughter Workbook: http://worksheets.kclanderson.com

Contact Information

Website: www.kclanderson.com

The Peaceful Daughter Facebook page: https://www.facebook.com/peacefuldaughter

Twitter: @KCLAnderson

Pinterest: KCLAnderson

ABOUT DIFFERENCE PRESS

difference press

Difference Press offers solopreneurs, including life coaches, healers, consultants, and community leaders, a comprehensive solution to get their books written, published, and promoted. A boutique-style alternative to self-publishing, Difference Press boasts a fair and easy-to-understand profit structure, low-priced author copies, and author-friendly contract terms. Its founder, Dr. Angela Lauria, has been bringing to life the literary ventures of hundreds of authors-in-transformation since 1994.

YOUR DELICIOUS BOOK

Your Delicious Book is a trailblazing program for aspiring authors who want to create a non-fiction book that becomes a platform for growing their business or communicating their message to the world in a way that creates a difference in the lives of others.

In a market where hundreds of thousands books are published every year and never heard from again, all of The Author Incubator participants have bestsellers that are actively changing lives and making a difference. The program, supported by quarterly Difference Press book-marketing summits, has a proven track record of helping aspiring authors write books that matter. Our team will hold your hand from idea to impact, showing you how to write a book, what elements must be present in your book for it to deliver the results you need, and how to meet the needs of your readers. We give you all the editing, design, and technical support you need to ensure a high-quality book published to the Kindle platform. Plus, authors in the program are connected to a powerful community of authors-in-transformation and published bestselling authors.

TACKLING THE TECHNICAL ASPECTS OF PUBLISHING

The comprehensive coaching, editing, design, publishing, and marketing services offered by Difference Press mean that your book will be edited by a pro, designed by an experienced graphic artist, and published digitally and in print by publishing industry experts. We handle all of the technical aspects of your book's creation so you can spend more of your time focusing on your business.

APPLY TO WRITE WITH US

To submit an application to our acquisitions team visit www.YourDeliciousBook.com.

OTHER BOOKS BY DIFFERENCE PRESS

Confessions of an Unlikely Runner: A Guide to Racing and Obstacle Courses for the Averagely Fit and Halfway Dedicated

by Dana L. Ayers

Matter: How to Find Meaningful Work That's Right for You and Your Family

by Caroline Greene

Reclaiming Wholeness: Letting Your Light Shine Even If You're Scared to Be Seen

by Kimberlie Chenoweth

The Well-Crafted Mom: How to Make Time for Yourself and Your Creativity within the Midst of Motherhood

by Kathleen Harper

Lifestyle Design for a Champagne Life: Find Out Why the Law of Attraction Isn't Working, Learn the Secret to Lifestyle Design, and Create Your Champagne Life

by Cassie Parks

No More Drama: How to Make Peace with Your Defiant Kid

by Lisa Cavallaro

The Nurse Practitioner's Bag: Become a Healer, Make a Difference, and Create the Career of Your Dreams

by Nancy Brook

Farm Girl Leaves Home: An American Narrative of Inspiration and Transformation

by Margaret Fletcher

Whoops! I Forgot to Achieve My Potential

by Maggie Huffman

Only 10s: Using Distraction to Get the Right Things Done

by Mark Silverman

The Inside Guide to MS: How to Survive a New Diagnosis When Your Whole Life Changes (And You Just Want to Go Home)

by Andrea Hanson

Lee & Me: What I Learned from Parenting a Child with Adverse Childhood Experiences

by Wendy Gauntner

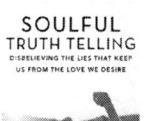

The Peaceful Daughter's Guide to Separating from A Difficult Mother: Freeing Yourself From The Guilt, Anger, Resentment and Bitterness

by Karen C. L. Anderson

Soulful Truth Telling: Disbelieving the Lies That Keep Us From the Love We Desire

by Sharon Pope

Personal Finance That Doesn't Suck: A 5-step Guide to Quit Budgeting, Start Wealth Building and Get the Most from Your Money

by Mindy Crary

The Cancer Whisperer: How to Let Cancer Heal Your Life

by Sophie Sabbage

CPSIA information can be obtained at www.ICGtesting.com
Printed in the USA
BVOW02s0817270516
449503BV00008B/105/P